## STECK-VAUGHN Spelling
### Linking Words to Meaning — LEVEL 2

**John R. Pescosolido**
Professor Emeritus
Central Connecticut State University
New Britain, Connecticut

## Reviewers

**Anita Uphaus**
Coordinator of Early Childhood Programs
Austin Independent School District
Austin, Texas

**Deanna Dove**
Education Specialist for Grades K–1
Orange County Public Schools
Orlando, Florida

**Patricia D'Amore**
Assistant Literacy Coordinator
Cooperative Educational Services
Trumbull, Connecticut

**Dr. Donna Ronzone**
Principal and Director of Special Education
Briggs Elementary School District
Santa Paula, California

STECK-VAUGHN
ELEMENTARY · SECONDARY · ADULT · LIBRARY
A Harcourt Company

www.steck-vaughn.com

# Acknowledgments

**Editorial Director** Stephanie Muller
**Senior Editor** Amanda Sperry
**Assistant Editor** Julie M. Smith
**Associate Director of Design** Cynthia Ellis
**Senior Design Manager** Cynthia Hannon
**Designer** Deborah Diver
**Media Researcher** Sarah Fraser
**Editorial Development, Design, and Production** The Quarasan Group, Inc.
**Cover Illustration** Dan Sharp
**Senior Technical Advisor** Alan Klemp

## PHOTO CREDITS

3 ©Andy Sacks/Stone; 5 ©Leonard L.T. Rhodes/Animals Animals; 6 ©Bob Daemmrich/The Image Works; 8 ©PhotoDisc, Inc.; 10 top (t) ©Claus Meyer/Black Star Publishing/PictureQuest; bottom left (bl) ©Fred Whitehead/Animals Animals; bottom right (br) ©Alan Oddie/PhotoEdit, Inc.; 11 (t) © PhotoDisc, Inc.; (b) ©Gary R. Zahm/DRK Photo; 12 ©Alan Oddie/PhotoEdit, Inc.; 14 ©PhotoDisc, Inc./EyeWire, Inc.; 18 ©PhotoDisc, Inc.; 20 ©Joe Towers/The Stock Market; 22-23 ©Tony Freeman/PhotoEdit, Inc.; 23 (t) ©Patrick Bennett/Corbis; (b) ©Mark Gibson/International Stock; 24 ©Tony Freeman/PhotoEdit, Inc.; 26 © Corel Corporation; 27 ©PhotoDisc, Inc.; 32 ©David Madison/Stone; 34 ©Gabe Palmer/The Stock Market; 35 ©Corbis; 36 ©Corbis; 38 (t) ©Raymond Gehman/Corbis; (b) ©PhotoDisc, Inc.; 39 ©PhotoDisc, Inc.; 41 ©Bob Rowan/Progressive Images/Corbis; 42 ©Peter Langone/International Stock; 46 ©Gillian Darley/Edifice/Corbis; 48 ©Stuart Westmorland/Stone; 50-51 (flowers) ©MetaTools, ©PhotoDisc, Inc.; 51 (l) ©Joe McDonald/Corbis; (r) ©Andy Sacks/Stone; 52 ©PhotoDisc, Inc.; 54 ©Digital Studios; 56-57 (leaves) ©PhotoDisc, Inc.; 56 ©Mary Kate Denny/PhotoEdit, Inc.; 57-58 ©David Young-Wolff/PhotoEdit/PictureQuest; 60 ©Fulvio Roiter/Corbis; 61 ©PhotoDisc, Inc.; 62 ©Bob Rowan/Progressive Image/Corbis; (apple) © Joe Atlas/Artville; (broccoli) ©PhotoDisc, Inc.; (coconut) ©PhotoDisc, Inc.; (orange) ©PhotoDisc, Inc.; (pepper) ©PhotoDisc, Inc.; 63 ©Bob Rowan/Progressive Image/Corbis; 64 ©PhotoDisc, Inc.; 66 ©Thomas Peterson/Stone; 68 (t) ©Steve Woit/Stock Boston/PictureQuest; (b) ©Miro Vintonir/Stock Boston/PictureQuest; 69 (t) ©Dewitt Jones/Corbis; (b) ©Scott McKiernan/Black Star Publishing/PictureQuest; 70 ©Miro Vintonir/Stock Boston/PictureQuest; 73 (t) ©MetaTools; (b) ©Michael Newman/PhotoEdit, Inc.; 74 (l) ©Artville; middle (m) ©PhotoDisc, Inc.; (r) ©Joe Atlas/Artville; 75 ©Bon/International Stock; 76 ©EyeWire, Inc.; 78 ©Rudi Von Briel/PhotoEdit, Inc.; 79 (t) ©Frank Lane Picture Agency/Corbis; (b) ©Charles Thatcher/Stone; 80 (t) ©Charles Thatcher/Stone; (b) ©Craig Hammell/The Stock Market; 81 ©Paul Barton/The Stock Market; 82 ©Charles Krebs/The Stock Market; 83 ©Geostock/PhotoDisc/PictureQuest; 86 ©Ronn Maratea/International Stock; 88 ©SuperStock, Inc.; 93 ©Corbis; 94 ©SuperStock, Inc.; 95 ©Bruce Miller/Corbis; 100 ©Terry Vine/Stone; ; 101 ©Corbis; 106 ©Quarasan; 107 ©Renee Lynn/Stone; 109 ©Tony Freeman/PhotoEdit/PictureQuest; 110 ©Sunstar/International Stock; 116 ©Joe Willis/International Stock; 122 ©Digital Studios; 123 ©Myrleen Ferguson/PhotoEdit, Inc.; 126 ©Dean Abramson/Stock Boston/PictureQuest; 128 ©Corbis; 134 ©Michael Newman/PhotoEdit, Inc.; 140 ©John & Lisa Merrill/Stone; 141 (t) ©RB Studio 97/The Stock Market; (b) ©LWA-JDC/The Stock Market; 142 ©Corbis; 143 ©PhotoDisc, Inc.; 144 ©Kent Miles/FPG International; 150 ©Barbara Von Hoffmann/Animals Animals; 151 ©PhotoDisc, Inc.; 156 ©Digital Studios; 157 (jar) ©Corbis; 157-162 ©PhotoDisc, Inc.; 163 ©Corbis; 164 (t) ©PhotoDisc, Inc.; 164 (fish) ©Leonard L.T. Rhodes/Animals Animals; 164 (water) ©MetaTools; 165 ©Ariel Skelley/The Stock Market; 166 ©Leonard L.T. Rhodes/Animals Animals; 168 ©Michael Newman/PhotoEdit, Inc.; 169 ©SuperStock, Inc.; 174 ©RubberBall Productions/PictureQuest; 175 ©PhotoDisc, Inc.; 177 ©Scott Barrow, Inc./International Stock; 178 ©Chris Jones/The Stock Market; 179 ©PhotoDisc, Inc.; 181 ©PhotoDisc, Inc.; 184 ©Corbis; 185 ©PhotoDisc, Inc.; 188 ©Yann Arthus-Bertrand/Corbis; 189 (tl) ©PhotoDisc, Inc.; (ml) ©PhotoDisc, Inc.; (bl) ©Digital Studios; (tr) ©Corbis; (mr) ©Digital Studios; (br) ©PhotoDisc, Inc.; 190 ©Corbis; 191 ©MetaTools; 196 ©PhotoDisc, Inc.; 197 ©Michael Rosenfeld/Stone; 202 ©Ariel Skelley/The Stock Market; 203 ©David Young-Wolff/PhotoEdit, Inc.; 204 (l) ©Bob Peterson/FPG International; (tr) ©Jose L. Pelaez/The Stock Market; (mr) ©Larry Edwards/Zuma/The Stock Market; (br) ©Corbis; 205 (t) ©Zigy Kaluzny/Stone; (m) ©SuperStock, Inc.; (b) ©Arnulf Husmo/Stone; 206 ©Corbis; 208 (l) ©TMC/Photo Network/PictureQuest; (r) ©Photodisc, Inc.; 209 ©SuperStock, Inc.; 211 ©PhotoDisc, Inc. Dictionary photos: 214 ©Superstock Inc.; 215 ©Jon Feingersh/The Stock Market; 217 ©E. Lettau/FPG International; 220 ©David M. Schleser/Nature's Images, Inc./Photo Researchers, Inc.; 222 ©George Schiavone/The Stock Market; 225 ©Gary Buss/FPG International; 226 ©Superstock, Inc.; 227 ©Stephen Wilkes/The Image Bank; 232 ©Superstock, Inc.; 233 ©Telegraph Colour Library/FPG International; 236 ©Superstock, Inc.; 239 ©FPG International. Additional dictionary photos by: Comstock Klips, Corbis, Corel Corporation, PhotoDisc, Inc., Steck-Vaughn Collection.

## ART CREDITS

Bernard Adnet 9; Marilynn G. Barr 16–18, 47, 129; Shirley Beckes 33; Mircea Catusanu 117, 145, 192–194; Randy Chewning 65, 87, 107, 111, 209; Shelley Dieterichs 39, 61, 208; Karen Dugan 13, 106, 124–126; Cecile Duray–Bito 44–46; Allan Eitzen 15, 146–148, 198–200; Cynthia Fisher 170–172; Ruth Flanigan 55, 112–114; Rusty Fletcher 21, 59; Dara Goldman 43; John Steven Gurney 130–132; Laurie Hamilton 77; Laura Jacobsen 90–92; Susan Jaekel 53, 67, 152–154; John Kanzler 4, 102–104; Brian Lies 31, 89, 174; Ben Mahan 25, 49, 135; Erin Mauterer 84–86; Sherry Neidigh 5, 186–188; Cary Pillo 96–98, 136–138, 175; Rebecca Thornburgh 118–120, 140; Dorothy Stott 158–160.

Pronunciation key and diacritical marks copyright © 1998 by Houghton Mifflin Company. Adapted and reproduced by permission from *The American Heritage Student Dictionary*.

*Steck-Vaughn Spelling: Linking Words to Meaning* is a registered trademark of Steck-Vaughn Company.

### ISBN 0-7398-3610-2

The words *bug, frog, pond,* and *snail* are hidden on the cover. Can you find them?

# Contents

# Unit 3

# Unit 4

# Unit 5

# Unit 6

# Study Steps to Learn a Word

**1** **Say** the word. What consonant sounds do you hear? What vowel sounds do you hear? How many syllables do you hear?

**2** **Look** at the letters in the word. Think about how each sound is spelled. Find any spelling patterns or parts that you know. Close your eyes. Picture the word in your mind.

**3** **Spell** the word aloud.

**4** **Write** the word. Say each letter as you write it.

**5** **Check** the spelling. If you did not spell the word correctly, use the study steps again.

Use the steps on this page to study words that are hard for you.

# Spelling Strategies

## What can you do when you aren't sure how to spell a word?

Say the word aloud. Make sure you say it correctly. Listen to the sounds in the word. Think about letters and patterns that might spell the sounds.

Look in the Spelling Table to find common spellings for sounds in the word.

Think about related words. They may help you spell the word you're not sure of.

longer—long

Guess the spelling of the word and check it in a dictionary.

Write the word in different ways. Compare the spellings and choose the one that looks correct.

tyger    tieger
tiger    tigher

Draw the shape of the word to help you remember its spelling.

thing

Choose a rhyming helper and use it. A rhyming helper is a word that rhymes with the word and is spelled like it.

fell—bell

Create a memory clue to help you remember the spelling.

Cold has the word old.

# Lesson 1

# Words with Short a

cat

**1. Beginning Short a**

_____

_____

_____

_____

_____

**2. Middle Short a**

_____

_____

_____

_____

_____

_____

_____

van
an
after
flat
hand
cat
and
has
am
than
add
man

## Say and Listen

Say each spelling word. Listen for the vowel sound you hear in van.

## Think and Sort

The vowel sound in van is called short a. All of the spelling words have the short a sound. It is spelled a. Spell each word aloud.

Look at the letters in each word. Is the short a at the beginning or in the middle of the word?

1. Write the **five** spelling words that have short a at the beginning.

2. Write the **seven** spelling words that have short a in the middle.

Use the steps on page 6 to study words that are hard for you.

### Spelling Patterns

The short a sound can be spelled a.

| add | van |
| --- | --- |

## Spelling and Meaning

**Clues**   Write the spelling word for each clue.

1. pet that meows                                    _____

2. part of an arm                                    _____

3. what you can do with numbers      _____

4. the opposite of **before**               _____

5. what a boy grows up to be            _____

**Letter Scramble**   Unscramble the letters in dark type
to make a spelling word. Write the word to complete the sentence.

6. **na**   I ate _____ apple.

7. **hant**   His friend is older _____ he is.

8. **ahs**   Rita is not here because she _____ a cold.

9. **ma**   You are tall, but I _____ short.

10. **latf**   The top of a table is _____.

11. **dna**   Sam likes blue _____ purple.

**W**ord Story   One spelling
word comes from the word
**caravan**. A long time ago, a
**caravan** was a covered carriage
or cart. Write the spelling word
that comes from **caravan**.

12. _____

**Family Tree: hand**   Think about
how the **hand** words are alike in
spelling and meaning. Then add
another **hand** word to the tree.

handing

handed

13.

handy

handle

hand

Use each spelling word once to complete the selection.

# To the Rescue!

Sometimes wild animals need help.  Storms destroy their home.  They get sick or hurt.  Their babies get lost.  Wildlife rescue groups can help these animals.  These groups take care of animals in special parks just for wildlife.  They do even more _____ care for the animals, though.  They also return some of them to their natural home _____ the animals are well or old enough.

1

2

What kinds of animals do wildlife rescue groups help?  They help any animal in need.  Most wildlife parks have raccoons _____ birds.  Some even have bobcats.  A bobcat is a wild _____.

3

4

Wildlife parks have trees that animals can climb. The parks also have _____ 5 places where animals can walk and run.

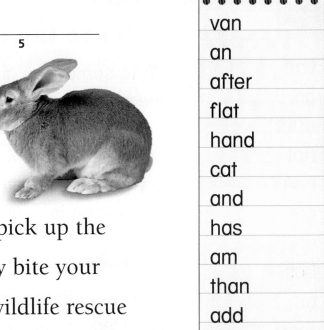

What should you do if you see _____ 6 animal in trouble? Do not try to pick up the animal. If you do, the animal may bite your _____ 7. Instead, call a wildlife rescue group. Your phone book _____ 8 names of rescue groups you can call. A _____ 9 or a woman will come to help. The worker will put the animal in a truck or a _____ 10 and take it to a wildlife park. People at the park will give the animal the care it needs. You can tell them to _____ 11 your name to their list of helpers.

Are you ready to become a rescue helper? If you are, say, "I _____ 12!"

van
an
after
flat
hand
cat
and
has
am
than
add
man

## Spelling and Writing

**Word list:**

van
an
after
flat
hand
cat
and
has
am
than
add
man

### Write to the Point

Write sentences about one of the animals at a wildlife park or a zoo. Tell what it looks like and other things you know about it. Try to use spelling words from this lesson in your writing.

Use the strategies on page 7 when you are not sure how to spell a word.

### Proofreading

Proofread the report below. Use proofreading marks to correct four spelling mistakes, one capitalization mistake, and one punctuation mistake.

**Proofreading Marks**
◯ spell correctly
≡ capitalize
⊙ add period

**Science Field Trip          Monday, October 3**

1. Where did you go?

we went to Lance Wildlife Park.

2. What did you see?

A mann held a baby bottle in his handd.

He fed a baby tiger We saw ane alligator swim.

3. What did you like best?

I liked the elephant best. I amm glad we went.

## Language Connection

**Capital Letters**   Use a capital letter to begin the first word of a sentence.

> **M**y cat climbs trees all the time.

Choose the correct word in dark type to complete each sentence. Then write the sentence correctly. Remember to begin the sentence with a capital letter.

1. my (**cat**, **and**) is stuck in a tree.

   _____

2. a (**flat**, **man**) comes to help.

   _____

3. he (**hand**, **has**) a ladder.

   _____

4. she jumps down (**after**, **and**) runs home.

   _____

## ⭐ Challenge Yourself

What do you think each Challenge Word means? Check the Spelling Dictionary to see if you are right. Then use the Challenge Words to write sentences on separate paper.

| Challenge Words |
| --- |
| active |
| blank |
| habit |

5. Monkeys and kangaroos are **active** animals.

6. Erase your answer and leave the box **blank**.

7. Brushing your teeth is a good **habit**.

# More Words with Short a

catch

**1. Beginning Short a**

_____

**2. Middle Short a**

_____
_____
_____
_____
_____
_____
_____
_____
_____
_____
_____

catch
fast
matter
have
land
that
back
last
thank
ask
sang
black

## Say and Listen

Say each spelling word. Listen for the short a sound.

## Think and Sort

All of the spelling words have the short a sound. It is spelled a. Spell each word aloud.

Look at the letters in each spelling word. Is the short a at the beginning or in the middle of the word?

1. Write the **one** word that has short a at the beginning.

2. Write the **eleven** words that have short a in the middle. One word has an e at the end, but the e is silent. Circle the word.

Use the steps on page 6 to study words that are hard for you.

## Spelling Patterns

The short a sound can be spelled a.

| ask | back | have |
|-----|------|------|

## Spelling and Meaning

**Word Groups**   Write the spelling word that belongs in each group.

1. danced, acted, _____

2. sea, sky, _____

3. orange, yellow, _____

4. throw, hit, _____

5. quick, swift, _____

6. had, has, _____

**Rhymes**   Write the spelling word that completes each sentence and rhymes with the underlined word.

7. Why did Dee _____ for that silly <u>mask</u>?

8. Hector wanted to _____ me for the piggy <u>bank</u>.

9. What is the _____ with the pancake <u>batter</u>?

10. Ming ran around the <u>track</u> and _____ home.

11. What is the name of _____ <u>cat</u>?

**W**ord Story   Long ago one of the spelling words was spelled **latost**. It meant "latest." Now it means "coming at the end." It has a different spelling, too. Write the word.

12. _____

**Family Tree: thank**  Think about how the **thank** words are alike in spelling and meaning. Then add another **thank** word to the tree.

thanked

thankful

thanking

13.

thank

Use each spelling word once to complete the story.

# The Violin Lesson

Ann's mother said she would be _____
1
at two o'clock. Ann picked up her violin case and got out
of the car. "It doesn't _____ if you're late," she
2
said. "I have a lot of practicing to do."

Ann watched her mother drive off. It was a beautiful

spring day. Children were playing

_____ and tag at the park.
3

A bird _____ above her head.
4

Ann watched the bird _____
5

near the feet of a girl. The girl was

older than Ann. She was carrying a

_____ violin case.
6

"Hi!" Ann called. "I _____ never
                           7
seen you here before. My name is Ann. I've
been taking lessons from Mr. Crabbe each week
for the _____ six months."
              8

"I start today," the tall girl said.

"Well, let me tell you about Mr. Crabbe.
He'll want you to practice a lot! I practice every
day. At first I could only play slow songs. Now
I can even play some really _____
                                        9
ones. I have Mr. Crabbe to _____ for
                                      10
being a good player. He's a very good teacher."

The tall girl smiled. "Do you know who
I am?" she asked Ann.

"No, I don't," Ann said. She hadn't thought
to _____ the girl's name.
        11

"I'm Tina Crabbe. Mr. Crabbe is my
grandfather," Tina said. "Thank you for saying
_____ he's a good teacher."
        12

Ann smiled. She said good-bye and went
inside for her lesson with Mr. Crabbe.

catch
fast
matter
have
land
that
back
last
thank
ask
sang
black

catch
fast
matter
have
land
that
back
last
thank
ask
sang
black

### Write to the Point

Ann plays the violin. What kind of musical instrument do you like? Write sentences about the instrument. Tell what you know about it and why you like it. Try to use spelling words from this lesson in your sentences.

Use the strategies on page 7 when you are not sure how to spell a word.

### Proofreading

Proofread the e-mail below. Use proofreading marks to correct four spelling mistakes, one capitalization mistake, and one punctuation mistake.

Proofreading Marks
⬭ spell correctly
≡ capitalize
⊙ add period

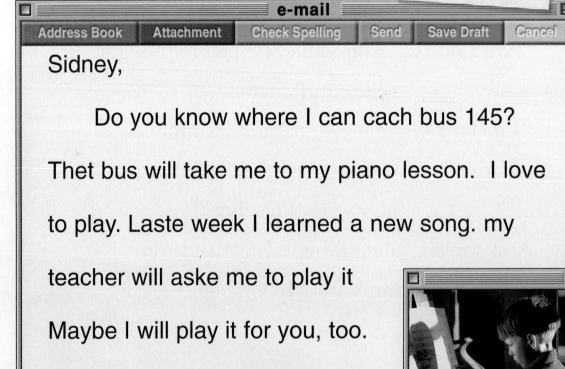

**e-mail**

| Address Book | Attachment | Check Spelling | Send | Save Draft | Cancel |

Sidney,

Do you know where I can cach bus 145?

Thet bus will take me to my piano lesson.  I love

to play. Laste week I learned a new song. my

teacher will aske me to play it

Maybe I will play it for you, too.

Max

## Language Connection

**Periods**  Use a period at the end of a sentence that tells something.

> Camels live in the desert**.**

Choose the word from the boxes that completes each sentence.
Then write the sentence correctly. Remember to put a period
at the end.

fast    back    land    have

1. A camel can carry people on its _____

_____

2. Some camels _____ one hump

_____

3. Camels can run _____

_____

4. They run across dry _____

_____

## Challenge Yourself

Use the Spelling Dictionary to answer these
questions. Then use the Challenge Words to write
sentences on separate paper.

**Challenge Words**

napkin

craft

cannon

5. Does a potter have a **craft**? _____

6. Do people use a **napkin** to clean their hands after a meal?

_____

7. Would you find a **cannon** in your kitchen? _____

# Words with Short e

jet

## 1. e Words

_____
_____
_____
_____
_____
_____
_____
_____
_____
_____

## 2. ay Word

_____

## 3. ai Word

_____

ten
when
bed
shelf
jet
yes
said
went
kept
says
next
end

## Say and Listen

Say each spelling word. Listen for the vowel sound you hear in ten.

## Think and Sort

The vowel sound in ten is called short e. All of the spelling words have the short e sound. Spell each word aloud.

Look at the letters in each word. Think about how short e is spelled.

1. Write the **ten** spelling words that have short e spelled e.

2. Write the **one** spelling word that has short e spelled ay.

3. Write the **one** spelling word that has short e spelled ai.

Use the steps on page 6 to study words that are hard for you.

### Spelling Patterns

The short e sound can be spelled e, ay, or ai.

| e | ay | ai |
|---|---|---|
| ten | says | said |

## Spelling and Meaning

**Word Math** Add and subtract letters and picture names. Write each spelling word.

1. b +  − sl = _____

2. sh + _____ = _____

3. w + _____ = _____

4. _____ − am + et = _____

5. _____ − p + d = _____

**Word Groups** Write the spelling word that belongs in each group.

6. near, beside, _____

7. told, asked, _____

8. saved, stored, _____

9. eight, nine, _____

10. no, maybe, _____

11. tells, asks, _____

**W**ord Story  Long ago one of the spelling words was spelled **wente**. It meant "did go." Its meaning hasn't changed, but its spelling has. Write the spelling that we use today.

12. _____

**Family Tree: end** Think about how the **end** words are alike in spelling and meaning. Then add another **end** word to the tree.

ends

ended

13.

unending

end

Use each spelling word once to complete the selection.

# Jet Travel

Long ago, travel could take days or weeks. When people needed to go far away, they usually _____ on
<u>1</u>
trains and ships. Over the years, travel _____
<u>2</u>
getting faster and faster. Today people can fly from one place to another on a _____.
<u>3</u>

What do you do _____ you travel on a jet?
<u>4</u>
The first thing you do is find your seat. A jet has many rows of seats. Some seats are _____ to windows.
<u>5</u>

You might need to store things that you have with you.
A closed-in _____ hangs above each row of seats.
<u>6</u>
People put things such as coats and small bags on the shelf.

Next, put on your seat belt and get ready for the trip.
Someone will tell about safety. Listen carefully. What that
person _____ is important. In case of an
<u>7</u>
emergency, you will want to remember what the person
showed you and _____ to do.
<u>8</u>
You will also hear the pilot speak. The pilot will tell
about the weather and the flight.

Someone might ask if you would like something to eat or drink. If you say _____9_____, you will get a snack or a meal. You might want to rest or sleep. A flight across the sea can last nine or _____10_____ hours—or more. Many people try to sleep on long trips. The seat leans back. It is almost as if you are lying in a _____11_____.

At the _____12_____ of the trip, the pilot will speak again. He or she will tell about the landing. The pilot and crew will also thank you for flying with them. They look forward to seeing you on your next trip!

ten
when
bed
shelf
jet
yes
said
went
kept
says
next
end

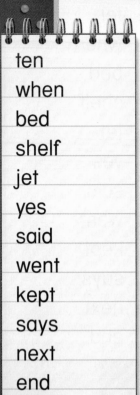

ten
when
bed
shelf
jet
yes
said
went
kept
says
next
end

## Write to the Point

You have read about plane travel. Now write about another way to travel. You may want to tell about traveling by bus, train, or car. Try to use spelling words from this lesson in your writing.

> Use the strategies on page 7 when you are not sure how to spell a word.

## Proofreading

Proofread the postcard below. Use proofreading marks to correct four spelling mistakes, one capitalization mistake, and one punctuation mistake.

Proofreading Marks
◯ spell correctly
≡ capitalize
⊙ add period

Dear Lan,

We wint on a train trip When the train turned a big corner, we saw the train car at the very ende! I slept in the top bed. ted slept in the bottom one. He sayd the sounds kept him awake. I slept great. I want you to come with us naxt time.

Love,

Fern

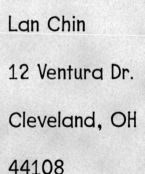

Lan Chin

12 Ventura Dr.

Cleveland, OH

44108

## Language Connection

**Sentences**   A sentence begins with a capital letter and ends with a period or other end mark. Unscramble each sentence and write it correctly.

**1.** ten cats my friend has

_____

**2.** hid they under the bed

_____

**3.** on a shelf they sat

_____

**4.** they toy played jet with a

_____

## ⭐ Challenge Yourself

What do you think each Challenge Word means? Check the Spelling Dictionary to see if you are right. Then use the Challenge Words to write sentences on separate paper.

> **Challenge Words**
>
> melon
>
> pedal
>
> method

**5.** The best **method** of brushing your teeth is brushing in circles.

**6.** My favorite fruit at the picnic was the **melon**.

**7.** My sister's bike needs a new **pedal**.

## Lesson 4
# More Words with Short e

bell

**1. e Words**

_____
_____
_____
_____
_____
_____
_____
_____
_____

**2. a Words**

_____
_____

best
well
any
seven
many
dress
desk
rest
bell
send
help
egg

## Say and Listen

Say each spelling word. Listen for the short e sound.

## Think and Sort

All of the spelling words have the short e sound. Spell each word aloud.

Look at the letters in each word. Think about how short e is spelled. How many spellings for short e do you see?

1. Write the **ten** spelling words that have short e spelled e.

2. Write the **two** spelling words that have short e spelled a.

Use the steps on page 6 to study words that are hard for you.

**Spelling Patterns**

The short e sound can be spelled e or a.

| e | a |
|------|------|
| desk | any |

## Spelling and Meaning

**Word Groups** Write the spelling word that belongs in each group.

1. five, six, _____

2. several, lots, _____

3. table, chair, _____

4. good, better, _____

5. one, every, _____

6. good, fine, _____

**What's Missing?** Write the missing spelling word.

7. the chicken and the _____

8. ring the _____

9. _____ an e-mail

10. _____ when you're tired

11. a woman's _____

**W**ord Story One of the spelling words comes from an old word that was spelled **hjalpa**. Then the spelling was changed to **helpen**. Write the spelling that we use today.

12. _____

**Family Tree: dress** Think about how the **dress** words are alike in spelling and meaning. Then add another **dress** word to the tree.

dressed

dresser     13.

dressing

dress

Use each spelling word once to complete the selection.

# Meg's Chickens

October 20

Dear Diary,

   Today is my birthday.  Tonight will be special.  My family and I will have a party.  We will have birthday cake and ice cream.  I will wear my best _____.
                                                                 1

   School was really special today.  Last week Grandpa said he would _____ me a surprise.  He sent me
                                      2
eight eggs to take to class.  Everyone wanted to see baby chicks being born.  The eggs hatched today.  What a surprise that was!

   My _____ is right by the eggs.  Right after
          3
the _____ for lunch rang, I looked in the box.
        4
I saw that one _____ was beginning to crack.
                        5

   Everyone ran to see the new chick.  One by one, the other _____ eggs began to crack.  Soon we
             6
could see all the babies. Then my friend Riley said, "I've never seen _____ chickens like those before!"
                  7

   "Where did you get the eggs?" my teacher asked.

"My grandfather gave them to me," I said.
"He wants to _____ me learn about the
8
animals on his farm."

My teacher laughed. "He likes to play jokes,
too," she said. The _____ of the class
9
also laughed. Not _____ things surprise
10
me. But the eight tiny turtles crawling around in
the box sure did!

When I left school, all the baby turtles were
doing _____. Everyone calls them Meg's
11
chickens. Grandpa gave me the _____
12
birthday surprise ever!

best
well
any
seven
many
dress
desk
rest
bell
send
help
egg

## Spelling and Writing

best
well
any
seven
many
dress
desk
rest
bell
send
help
egg

### Write to the Point

Meg wrote about her special day in her diary. Start your own diary. Write three or four sentences about a special day you have had. Begin with "Dear Diary." Try to use spelling words from this lesson in your sentences.

**Use the strategies on page 7 when you are not sure how to spell a word.**

### Proofreading

Proofread the diary page below. Use proofreading marks to correct four spelling mistakes, one capitalization mistake, and one punctuation mistake.

**Proofreading Marks**
○ spell correctly
≡ capitalize
? add question mark

Dear Diary,

What will I do with so meny baby turtles Grandfather can take sevan. Riley says she does not want eny. I asked Mom if I could keep just one. that is the bist idea. She says I can. I will take good care of my baby turtle. That's all for today.

## Using the Spelling Table

A spelling table can help you find a word in a dictionary. It shows different spellings for a sound. Suppose you are not sure how to spell the last sound in **pick**. Is it **c**, **k**, **ch**, or **ck**? First, find the sound and the example words in the table. Then read the first spelling for the sound and look up **pic** in the dictionary. Look for each spelling in the dictionary until you find the correct one.

| Sound | Example Words | Spellings |
|-------|---------------|-----------|
| k | can, keep, school, sick | c  k  ch ck |

Use the Spelling Table on page 213 and the Spelling Dictionary to write the missing letters in the picture names.

1.  _____ ity

2.  bla _____

3.  _____ ale

4.  s _____ ool

5.  mou _____ e

6.  sn _____ l

## Challenge Yourself

Decide which Challenge Word fits each clue. Check the Spelling Dictionary to see if you are right. Then use the Challenge Words to write sentences on separate paper.

Challenge Words
beggar
tread
memory

7. A good one will help you in school. _____

8. This is someone who begs. _____

9. When you walk on something, you do this. _____

# Lesson 5

# People Words

girls

**1. Three Letters**

_____
_____
_____
_____
_____

**2. More Than Three Letters**

_____
_____
_____
_____
_____
_____

had
class
him
you
children
boys
our
girls
the
them
her
child

## Say and Listen

Say the spelling words. Listen to the sounds in each word.

## Think and Sort

Look at the letters in each word. Think about how each sound in the word is spelled. Spell each word aloud.

1. Write the **six** spelling words that have three letters.

2. Write the **six** spelling words that have more than three letters.

Use the steps on page 6 to study words that are hard for you.

| Three Letters | More Than Three Letters |
|---------------|-------------------------|
| him | boys |
| | child |
| | children |

## Spelling and Meaning

**Letter Scramble** Unscramble the letters in dark type to make a spelling word. Write the word to complete the sentence.

1. **hmet** The lions have their cubs with _____.

2. **reh** That is _____ new dress.

3. **hte** I saw a baby bird at _____ park.

4. **lascs** My _____ went to the zoo.

5. **cdlnerhi** Young people are called _____.

6. **lihdc** The little _____ had a toy boat.

7. **rou** Four people will fit in _____ car.

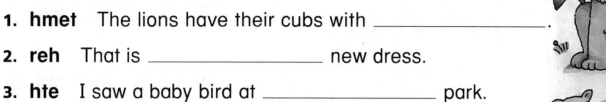

**Rhymes** Write the spelling word that completes each sentence and rhymes with the underlined word.

8. Do you know what <u>Dad</u> _____?

9. Those two _____ have lots of <u>toys</u>.

10. Happy birthday <u>to</u> _____!

11. Did you see _____ <u>swim</u>?

**W**ord Story One spelling word comes from the old word **gyrle.** Long ago **gyrle** meant "child." The spelling word names one kind of children. Write the spelling word.

12. _____

**Family Tree: you** Think about how the **you** words are alike in spelling and meaning. Then add another **you** word to the tree.

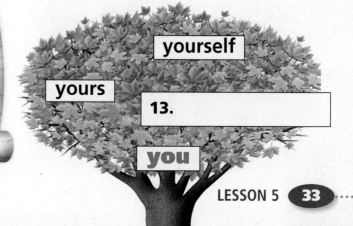

yourself

yours

13.

you

Use each spelling word once to complete the selection.

# Classrooms of Long Ago

Look around your classroom. How many students do you see? Is each _____ about _____
1                                              2
same age? Today _____ idea of school is a
3
building with many classrooms. All the students in each
_____ are close to the same age. It was not
4
this way long ago. Back then, _____ of many
5
ages learned together. Students studied in a one-room
school. What was school like for _____?
6

Students often began the school day with greetings.
The _____ often bowed to the teacher. The
7
_____ often curtsied.
8

Students worked hard at their lessons. They learned to read and to do math. They learned facts and said them over and over. They learned to write neatly. Few students _____ pen and paper.
9

They wrote on thin, flat stones called slates.
They also used pencils made from slate.

At the end of the school day, there were jobs
to do. The teacher often asked students to help
_____ or _____. Students
      10               11
sometimes wiped the blackboards. They
brought in wood for the next day's fire.

Think about schools of long
ago. Then think about your
school. Would _____
                12
like to learn in a one-room
school? Or would you rather
learn in your school?

had
class
him
you
children
boys
our
girls
the
them
her
child

had
class
him
you
children
boys
our
girls
the
them
her
child

### Write to the Point

What does your class do every day? Write sentences that tell about the things you do at school. Try to use spelling words from this lesson in your sentences.

Use the strategies on page 7 when you are not sure how to spell a word.

### Proofreading

Proofread the journal page below. Use proofreading marks to correct four spelling mistakes, one capitalization mistake, and one punctuation mistake.

Proofreading Marks
◯ spell correctly
≡ capitalize
⊙ add period

September 2

Today was my first day at Pine School.

I had fun. My clas has twenty childrin.

There are three new gurls, counting me

I played tag with Ellie and Adam at

recess. when the bell rang, I knew I had

made new friends. Owr teacher seems

nice, too!

## Dictionary Skills

**ABC Order** Look at the Spelling Dictionary. The first word is **active**. The last word is **zoo**. The words in a dictionary are in ABC order. This order is also called alphabetical order.

Write the missing letters in the alphabet.

a b c d e f g h i j k l m

n o p q r s t u v w x y z

Write these words in alphabetical order.

them    boys    him    you    class    girls

1. _____  2. _____

3. _____  4. _____

5. _____  6. _____

## Challenge Yourself

Write the Challenge Word for each clue. Check the Spelling Dictionary to see if you are right. Then use the Challenge Words to write sentences on separate paper.

**Challenge Words**
pupil
classmate
buddy

7. This is a word for a close friend. _____

8. This is a student or a part of the eye. _____

9. This names someone in your class. _____

# Unit 1 Review
## Lessons 1–5

Use the steps on page 6 to study words that are hard for you.

**1**

am
after
than
hand

## Words with Short **a**

Write the spelling word that completes each sentence.

1. Look at the shell in my _____.

2. I _____ going to have strawberry jam.

3. What did they want to do _____ the show?

4. I ran faster _____ James did.

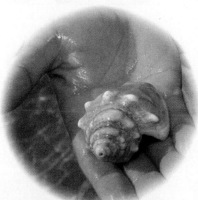

**2**

ask
have
catch
that

## More Words with Short **a**

Unscramble the letters in dark type to make a spelling word. Then write the word to complete the sentence.

5. **hatt**   Is _____ your puppy?

6. **ska**   Let's _____ them to come with us.

7. **avhe**   Did you _____ fun at the pool?

8. **tchac**   I can _____ a football.

**3**

kept
when
says
said

## Words with Short e

Write the spelling word for each definition.

9. speaks _____

10. stored _____

11. at what time _____

12. talked _____

 **4**

seven
egg
many
any

## More Words with Short e

Write the spelling word for each clue.

13. This is what a baby bird comes from.

_____

14. You have this when you have a lot

of things. _____

15. This is one of several. _____

16. Four and three make this. _____

**5**

our
you
girls
children

## People Words

Write the missing spelling word.

17. a cake for me and _____

18. games for boys and _____

19. mothers and their _____

20. your team and _____ team

## 21. Short a Words

_____

_____

_____

_____

## 22. Words with Short e Spelled e

_____

_____

_____

_____

## 23. Word with Short e Spelled ay

_____

## 24. Word with Short e Spelled ai

_____

## 25. Words with Short e Spelled a

_____

_____

**Review Sort**

| seven | that | catch | egg |
| said | says | kept | any |
| have | when | many | after |

**21.** Write the **four** spelling words that have short a.

**22.** Write the **four** spelling words that have short e spelled e.

**23.** Write the **one** spelling word that has short e spelled ay.

**24.** Write the **one** spelling word that has short e spelled ai.

**25.** Write the **two** spelling words that have short e spelled a.

These four words have been sorted into two groups. Tell how the words in each group are alike.

**26. class     had**

_____

_____

**27. egg     bed**

_____

_____

# Writer's Workshop

## A Personal Narrative

A personal narrative is a story about you. A personal narrative has words like **I**, **me**, **we**, and **my**. Here is part of Elena's personal narrative.

### Snowball

This is how I met Snowball, my cat. It was a very cold day. It snowed all morning. After lunch I went outside to play. I walked down the hill. Then I heard a soft little cry. I looked all around. A little white kitten was hiding under a bush.

**Prewriting**  To write her personal narrative, Elena began with a chain of events chart. In the chart, she listed all the important things that happened. She listed these events in time order. Take a look at what Elena did.

| **1** | **2** |
|---|---|
| I went outside to play. | I walked down the hill. |

| **3** | **4** |
|---|---|
| I heard a little cry. | I found a kitten. |

## It's Your Turn!

Write your own personal narrative. It can be about any special time in your life. Begin by making a chain of events chart. Then follow the other steps in the writing process—writing, revising, proofreading, and publishing. Try to use spelling words in your personal narrative.

# Words with Short i

ship

## Say and Listen

Say each spelling word. Listen for the vowel sound you hear in big.

## Think and Sort

The vowel sound you hear in big is called short i. All the spelling words have the short i sound. Spell each word aloud.

Look at the letters in each word. Think about how short i is spelled.

1. **Three Letters**

_____
_____
_____
_____

2. **Four Letters**

_____
_____
_____
_____
_____
_____
_____

3. **Five Letters**

_____

big
ship
will
six
fill
hill
this
wind
pick
his
hid
trick

1. Write the **four** spelling words that have three letters.

2. Write the **seven** spelling words that have four letters.

3. Write the **one** spelling word that has five letters.

Use the steps on page 6 to study words that are hard for you.

### Spelling Patterns

The short i sound can be spelled i.

| big | ship | trick |

## Spelling and Meaning

**Clues**   Write the spelling word for each clue.

1. something you can climb    _____

2. a big boat    _____

3. to play a joke on someone    _____

4. the number after five    _____

5. what makes a kite fly    _____

**Rhymes**   Write the spelling word that completes each sentence and rhymes with the underlined word.

6. <u>Jill</u>, please _____ my glass with water.

7. Luis said <u>that</u> _____ hat is lost.

8. That <u>wig</u> is too _____ for my head.

9. <u>Mick</u> will _____ an apple from that tree.

10. I will <u>miss</u> riding _____ pony.

11. Marco _____ <u>still</u> be here tomorrow.

**Word Story**   Long ago the Old English word **hydan** meant "to cover." Over time the spelling changed to **hiden**. One spelling word comes from **hiden**. It means "kept out of sight." Write the spelling word.

12. _____

**Family Tree: fill**   Think about how the **fill** words are alike in spelling and meaning. Then add another **fill** word to the tree.

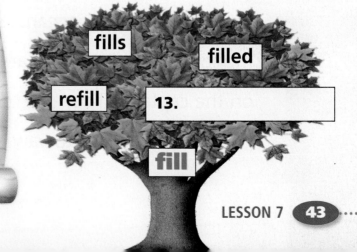

fills

filled

refill

13.

fill

Use each spelling word once to complete the selection.

# Sail Away!

People have used boats since early times. At first people rowed the boats. Then they added sails. The _____ blew against the sails and made the boats move.

1

Over time, people needed larger boats. These boats could carry more goods and people. A large boat was called a _____. Most ships were very _____.

2                                    3

Ships needed five or _____ sails in order to move.

4

Many men worked on a ship. The captain was the leader. One of his jobs was to _____ the crew that sailed

5

the ship.

Many captains and their crews sailed across the seas. They bought tea, spices, and cloth. Their goal was to _____ the ship with things they bought. Then they

6

sailed back home and sold the goods. Ships also carried travelers across the ocean. Some people did not have the money to pay the ship's fare. They played a _____

7

on the captain. They _____ on the ship. These

8

people were called stowaways.

Life on a sailing ship was hard. The food was not good. At times there was little fresh water. Great storms often came up suddenly. A wave in a big storm at sea might be as tall as a giant _____. People often got sick. When bad things happened, the captain tried to help people. It was part of _____ job.

> 9

> 10

After hundreds of years, people stopped using wind to power their ships. Instead, they began using steam engines. On _____ type of ship, people could travel faster. What kinds of ships do you think people _____ use in the future?

> 11

> 12

big
ship
will
six
fill
hill
this
wind
pick
his
hid
trick

## Spelling and Writing

big
ship
will
six
fill
hill
this
wind
pick
his
hid
trick

### Write to the Point

Write sentences about traveling by ship. Tell why you would or would not like it. Try to use spelling words from this lesson in your sentences.

Use the strategies on page 7 when you are not sure how to spell a word.

### Proofreading

Proofread the e-mail below. Use proofreading marks to correct four spelling mistakes, one capitalization mistake, and one punctuation mistake.

**Proofreading Marks**
◯ spell correctly
≡ capitalize
⊙ add period

---

**e-mail**

| Address Book | Attachment | Check Spelling | Send | Save Draft | Cancel |

Hi, Jason!

I just got a new model ship. Now I have sixe

If I had to pik my favorite one, it would be the

sailing ship. it is very big. The sails really work, too.

When the winde hits them, they fil with air. The ship

looks great sailing on the water!

What is your favorite kind of ship?

Ryan

# Language Connection

**Question Marks**   Use a question mark at
the end of a sentence that asks a question.

> What is the biggest animal in the world**?**
> Where is it found**?**

Choose the correct word in dark type to complete
each question. Then write the question correctly.
Remember to end it with a question mark.

1. How (**big**, **pick**) is a blue whale

   _____

2. Is it as large as a (**ship**, **six**)

   _____

3. What does (**this**, **trick**) animal eat

   _____

4. Can you see (**hid**, **his**) tail

   _____

## Challenge Yourself

What do you think each Challenge Word means?
Check the Spelling Dictionary to see if you are
right. Then use the Challenge Words to write
sentences on separate paper.

| Challenge Words |
| --- |
| admit |
| blizzard |
| glimpse |

5. We got a **glimpse** of the baby deer. Then it
   was gone.

6. Did she **admit** that she left the door open?

7. School was closed because of the **blizzard**.

# More Words with Short i

fish

**1. Four Letters**

_____
_____
_____
_____
_____
_____
_____

**2. Five Letters**

_____
_____
_____

**3. Six Letters**

_____
_____

ring
give
fish
think
thing
wish
spring
with
live
sister
swim
bring

## Say and Listen

Say each spelling word. Listen for the short i sound.

## Think and Sort

All of the spelling words have the short i sound. Spell each word aloud.

Look at the letters in each word. Think about how short i is spelled.

1. Write the **seven** spelling words that have four letters. Two of the words with four letters have an e at the end, but the e is silent. Circle the words.

2. Write the **three** spelling words that have five letters.

3. Write the **two** spelling words that have six letters.

Use the steps on page 6 to study words that are hard for you.

## Spelling Patterns

The short i sound can be spelled i.

| fish | give | think | spring |
|------|------|-------|--------|

## Spelling and Meaning

**Rhymes**   Write the spelling word that completes each sentence and rhymes with the underlined word.

1. Birds <u>sing</u> in the _____.

2. The fried _____ was on the <u>dish</u>.

3. The <u>king</u> wore a shiny gold _____.

4. I _____ Ben is at the skating <u>rink</u>.

5. Please _____ us some <u>string</u> for the kite.

**Word Meanings**   Write the spelling word for each meaning. Use the Spelling Dictionary if you need to.

6. to hope for something                                  _____

7. to hand something over                              _____

8. a girl with the same parents as another child    _____

9. an object                                                    _____

10. to move through water                              _____

11. having                                                        _____

**W**ord Story   Long ago the word that means "to have life" was spelled **lifen**. Over time the spelling changed. Write the spelling word that shows how **lifen** is spelled today.

12. _____

**Family Tree: fish**   Think about how the **fish** words are alike in spelling and meaning. Then add another **fish** word to the tree.

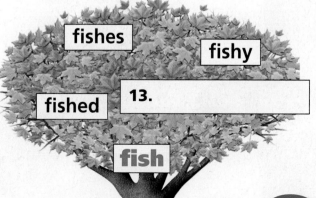

fishes

fishy

fished

13.

fish

Use each spelling word once to complete the selection.

# Spring Changes

Do you _____ in a place that has
1
long, cold winters? During months of ice and
snow, many people _____ for warmer
2
weather. They would _____ anything
3
to see flowers budding on trees. They are ready
for the long winter to end and for _____ to
4
begin. They know that spring will _____
5
warm, sunny days.

Spring brings many changes to land animals. Moles
and bats have slept for most of the winter. They have not
had a _____ to eat for weeks. They are very
6
hungry. They wake up and look for food.

Many baby animals are born in
the spring. Some animal parents
take care of their babies.

The babies learn to play _____ each
7
other. It's fun to watch a brother squirrel chase
his _____. The young animals run and
8
play with other family members, too.

The kind of _____ called salmon
9
do something special in the spring. They
_____ upstream. They do this to
10
get back to the place where they hatched.
There the fish lay their own eggs.

Spring is a happy time. Some
people _____ spring is the
11
best time of the year. They love to
hear a robin's song _____
12
through the air. What do you think?

ring
give
fish
think
thing
wish
spring
with
live
sister
swim
bring

ring
give
fish
think
thing
wish
spring
with
live
sister
swim
bring

### Write to the Point

Many people love spring. Write about your favorite season. Tell what you like best about it. Try to use spelling words from this lesson in your writing.

Use the strategies on page 7 when you are not sure how to spell a word.

### Proofreading

Proofread this paragraph from a newspaper article. Use proofreading marks to correct four spelling mistakes, one capitalization mistake, and one punctuation mistake.

**Proofreading Marks**
◯ spell correctly
≡ capitalize
? add question mark

Vegetables
Finest Quality Seeds

Flowers
Finest Quality Seeds

It is time to plant gardens! First, thnk about what you want to plant. Do you want to grow flowers or vegetables Then head out to your yard. Brang your shovel witt you. it is the best thinge for getting the soil ready for seeds.

## Dictionary Skills

**ABC Order**  When two words begin with the same letter, use the second letter to put the words in alphabetical order. Look at the words in the box. **Bell** comes before **big** because **e** comes before **i** in the alphabet.

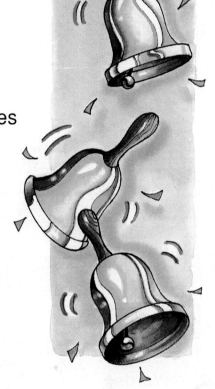

| bell     big |
|---|

Read each pair of words. Write the word that comes first in ABC order.

1. swim, sister  _____

2. got, give  _____

3. ring, run  _____

4. luck, live  _____

5. spring, stick  _____

6. thing, trick  _____

7. woman, wish  _____

## Challenge Yourself

What do you think each Challenge Word means? Check the Spelling Dictionary to see if you are right. Then use the Challenge Words to write sentences on separate paper.

**Challenge Words**
bitter
guilt
liberty

8. This coffee tastes **bitter**.

9. The man admitted his **guilt**.

10. Give the snake its **liberty** after you take it to Show and Tell.

# Words with Short o

block

## 1. o Words

_____
_____
_____
_____
_____
_____
_____
_____
_____
_____

## 2. a Words

_____
_____

| hot |
| what |
| dot |
| not |
| block |
| was |
| job |
| jog |
| top |
| on |
| hop |
| got |

## Say and Listen

Say each spelling word. Listen for the vowel sound you hear in hot.

## Think and Sort

The vowel sound you hear in hot is called short o. All the spelling words have the short o sound. Spell each word aloud.

Look at the letters in each word. Think about how short o is spelled. How many spellings for short o do you see?

1. Write the **ten** spelling words that have short o spelled o.

2. Write the **two** spelling words that have short o spelled a.

Use the steps on page 6 to study words that are hard for you.

### Spelling Patterns

The short o sound can be spelled o or a.

| o | a |
|---|---|
| dot | was |

## Spelling and Meaning

**Word Groups**  Write the spelling word that belongs in each group.

1. run, trot, _____

2. cold, warm, _____

3. skip, jump, _____

4. spot, mark, _____

5. work, chore, _____

6. town, street, _____

7. took, grabbed, _____

**Presto Change-O**  Change the order of each word in dark type to make a spelling word. Write the spelling word to complete the sentence.

8. **no**  Please turn _____ the light.

9. **ton**  Do _____ touch the oven!

10. **thaw**  Please tell me _____ this is.

11. **saw**  Who _____ at the door?

**W**ord Story  One very old word, **tuppaz**, meant "the highest point." The meaning of this word is the same today, but the spelling is different. Write the spelling that we use today.

12. _____

**Family Tree: hop**  Think about how the **hop** words are alike in spelling and meaning. Then add another **hop** word to the tree.

hops

hopping

13.

hopper

hop

Use each spelling word once to complete the selection.

# You Can Make Money!

Do you think you are too young to make money? That is _____ true at all. Are you wondering _____ you can do to earn money? Here are some ideas.

1

2

Walking dogs is a good way to make money. Ask a grownup to go with you when you walk a dog. Then be sure to stay _____ the sidewalk. Dress for the _____ and the weather. Wear something that you can move around in easily. Wear warm clothes if it is cold. Wear cool clothing if it is _____.

3

4

5

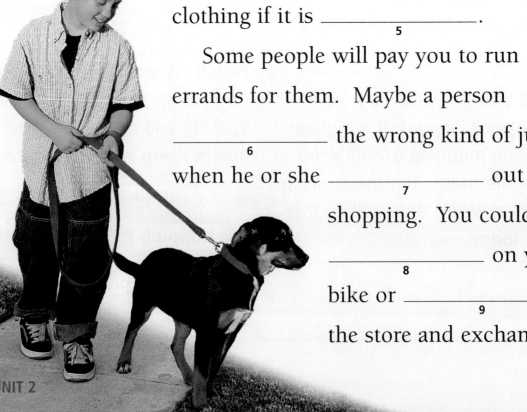

Some people will pay you to run errands for them. Maybe a person _____ the wrong kind of juice when he or she _____ out shopping. You could _____ on your bike or _____ to the store and exchange it.

6

7

8

9

Be sure you have a basket on your bike or wear a backpack. Try to work for people who live near you or even on the same city _____. That way, you will never be too
10
far from home.

You can also help people do things that are hard for them. Some people have trouble waking up in the morning. You could call them on the phone. Some people do not like to water their garden or rake leaves. You can do it for them.

Now are you ready to earn some money? Make a list of things you would like to do. Which is your favorite? Put it at the _____ of your list.
11
Talk to a grownup about the job you want to try. Then let people know you want work.

There is an old saying that you should _____ every *i* and
12
cross every *t*. That is another way of saying that you should do your best. If you plan well and do a good job, you may soon be earning money and have cash in your pocket. Good luck!

hot
what
dot
not
block
was
job
jog
top
on
hop
got

## Spelling and Writing

**Word list:**
- hot
- what
- dot
- not
- block
- was
- job
- jog
- top
- on
- hop
- got

### Write to the Point

Think of a job you can do. Then write sentences that tell other people about you. Try to make them want to hire you. Try to use spelling words from this lesson in your sentences.

Use the strategies on page 7 when you are not sure how to spell a word.

### Proofreading

Proofread the sign below. Use proofreading marks to correct four spelling mistakes, one capitalization mistake, and one punctuation mistake.

Proofreading Marks
- ◯ spell correctly
- ＝ capitalize
- ⊙ add period

Jason's Pet Care

do you have a cat or a dog? I can care for it when you are nat home My name is Jason White. I live un this blok. My phone number is 723-4100. Call and tell me wat you need. I will give you a good price.  I will also take great care of your pet.

## Language Connection

**Capital Letters**   Use a capital letter for the word **I** and to begin the names of people and pets.

Choose the correct word in dark type to complete each sentence. Then write the sentence. Remember to use capital letters.

**1.** corey jones wanted to go for a (**jog**, **got**).

_____

**2.** He and i ran around the (**block**, **dot**).

_____

**3.** i saw rusty (**top**, **hop**) on the porch.

_____

**4.** She (**not**, **got**) the paper.

_____

**5.** rusty (**was**, **what**) running fast.

_____

## Challenge Yourself

Use the Spelling Dictionary to answer these questions. Then use the Challenge Words to write sentences on separate paper.

| Challenge Words |
| --- |
| lobster |
| adopt |
| monster |

**6.** Does a **lobster** wear sneakers on its feet?   _____

**7.** Would a grownup **adopt** another grownup?   _____

**8.** Do scary movies sometimes have a **monster** in them?

_____

# More Words with Short o

ox

## 1. o Words

_____
_____
_____
_____
_____
_____
_____
_____
_____
_____

## 2. a Words

_____
_____

box
wash
rock
spot
want
drop
clock
stop
chop
ox
pond
shop

## Say and Listen

Say each spelling word. Listen for the short o sound.

## Think and Sort

All of the spelling words have the short o sound. Spell each word aloud.

Look at the letters in each word. Think about how short o is spelled. How many spellings for short o do you see?

1. Write the **ten** spelling words that have short o spelled o.

2. Write the **two** spelling words that have short o spelled a.

Use the steps on page 6 to study words that are hard for you.

## Spelling Patterns

The short o sound can be spelled o or a.

| o | a |
|---|---|
| shop | want |

## Spelling and Meaning

**Word Groups**   Write the spelling word that belongs in each group.

1. time, watch, _____

2. wish, need, _____

3. wait, quit, _____

4. cut, slice, _____

5. cow, horse, _____

6. ocean, lake, _____

7. clean, scrub, _____

**More Than One Meaning**   Some words have more than one meaning. Complete each pair of sentences with the correct spelling word.

8. We like to _____ at that store.

   I buy my skates at a sports _____.

9. There's a dirty _____ on my dress.

   Put the book in that _____.

10. I just felt a _____ of rain.

   That glass will break if you _____ it.

11. I found this _____ in my back yard.

   Will you _____ the baby?

**W**ord Story   One spelling word comes from the Greek word **pyxis**. **Pyxis** was the name of a kind of tree. People used the wood from the tree to make something that could hold things. Write the spelling word that comes from **pyxis**.

12. _____

**Family Tree: want**   Think about how the **want** words are alike in spelling and meaning. Then add another **want** word to the tree.

wanted

unwanted

wants

13.

want

Use each spelling word once to complete the selection.

# At the Supermarket

People push shopping carts around a big store. They look at shelves as they walk along. They see something they _____ 1 to buy, and they _____ 2 their cart. They pick up a can, a bag, or a _____. Then they 3 _____ it into the cart. 4

Where are these people? In a supermarket, of course! Many people _____ for food there each day. You 5 can buy regular foods in a supermarket, such as bread, milk, and eggs. But some supermarkets sell unusual foods, too.

In the produce section, you might see strange vegetables and fruits. You might see fruit shaped like a star. One kind of fruit is brown, hairy, and as hard as a _____. 6 That fruit is a coconut.

If you visit the meat section, you might find many kinds of meat. You may find buffalo meat or the tail of an _____. What can you see in a fish section? 7

You can see swordfish from the sea. You might see crawfish from a lake or a _____.
8

Some large stores sell more than just food. They also sell fresh flowers and even fancy soap to _____ your face.
9

Some supermarkets have a place for cooking shows. It is a favorite _____ for many
10
people. You can see cooks peel, _____,
11
and cook food. Then you get to taste the food.

A supermarket is a very interesting place to shop. Be sure to check the _____
12
often when you go. With so many things to see and do, you could lose track of time!

box
wash
rock
spot
want
drop
clock
stop
chop
ox
pond
shop

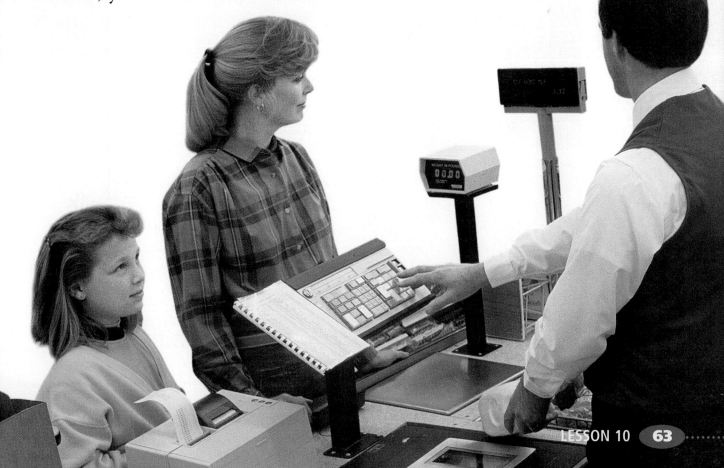

box
wash
rock
spot
want
drop
clock
stop
chop
ox
pond
shop

## Write to the Point

Do you help your family shop for food? Make a shopping list. Write four or five things you want to buy at the store. Try to use spelling words from this lesson in your list.

Use the strategies on page 7 when you are not sure how to spell a word.

## Proofreading

Proofread the note below. Use proofreading marks to correct four spelling mistakes, one capitalization mistake, and one punctuation mistake.

**Proofreading Marks**

◯ spell correctly

≡ capitalize

? add question mark

Mom,

Can we go shopping at the new supermarket today? We need some soap to wosh our hands. i would like a bax of cereal. Can I have the kind with nuts  Maybe we can shopp for a new clok, too. Dad says he wants one with big numbers.

milk
eggs
bread
fruit
soup

## Dictionary Skills

**Word Meanings**   The dictionary entry for a word gives its meaning.

> **ox** *plural* **oxen.** A male animal of the cattle family. *A strong ox is a useful farm animal.* ← **meaning**

Write the word from the boxes that names each picture. Then find each word in the Spelling Dictionary. Complete the meaning for the word.

| pond | ox | spot | rock |

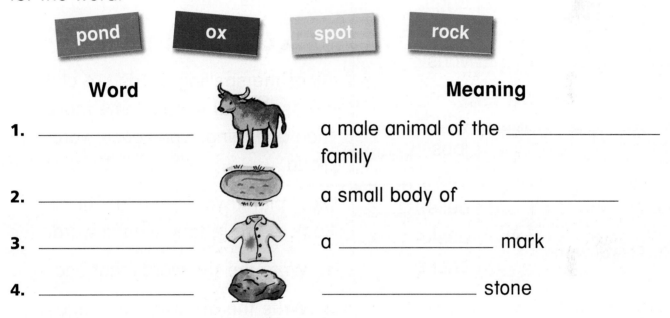

**Word**                                                                    **Meaning**

1. _____     a male animal of the _____ family

2. _____     a small body of _____

3. _____     a _____ mark

4. _____     _____ stone

## ⭐ Challenge Yourself

Write the Challenge Word for each clue. Check the Spelling Dictionary to see if you are right. Then use the Challenge Words to write sentences on separate paper.

**Challenge Words**
- profit
- dodge
- bonnet

5. This word means "move away quickly." _____

6. A store owner wants this to be big. _____

7. This kind of hat can be worn on a windy day. _____

# Plural Words

cats

## 1. Plurals with s

_____

_____

_____

_____

_____

_____

_____

_____

_____

## 2. Plural with es

_____

## 3. Other Plural

_____

men
dresses
eggs
ships
vans
cats
hands
jobs
jets
bells
desks
backs

## Say and Listen

Say the spelling words. Listen to the ending sounds.

## Think and Sort

All of the spelling words are plural words. **Plural** words name more than one thing. Spell each word aloud.

Most plural words end in s or es. Look at the letters in each word.

1. Write the **ten** words that end in s.

2. Write the **one** word that ends in es.

3. Write the **one** word that does not end in s or es.

Use the steps on page 6 to study words that are hard for you.

### Spelling Patterns

Most plurals are formed by adding s or es. A few plurals are formed in other ways.

| s | es | |
|---|---|---|
| hands | dresses | men |

## Spelling and Meaning

**Clues**   Write the spelling word for each clue.

1. what women wear   _____

2. things to ring   _____

3. big boats   _____

4. what chickens lay   _____

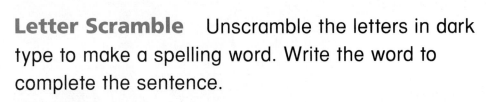

**Letter Scramble**   Unscramble the letters in dark type to make a spelling word. Write the word to complete the sentence.

5. **navs**   The school _____ have ten seats.

6. **bosj**   Both my brothers have _____.

7. **cabks**   These chairs have tall _____.

8. **nem**   Those _____ are my uncles.

9. **shand**   My _____ are in my pockets.

10. **tejs**   Two _____ flew across the sky.

11. **kedss**   We sit at the _____ in our classroom.

**W**ord Story   One spelling word is **chats** in French. In Italian it is **gatti**. In German it is **katzen**. It names one group of animals that people keep as pets. Long ago it was often spelled **cattes**. Write the spelling word.

12. _____

**Family Tree: ships**   Ships is a form of **ship**. Think about how the **ship** words are alike in spelling and meaning. Then add another **ship** word to the tree.

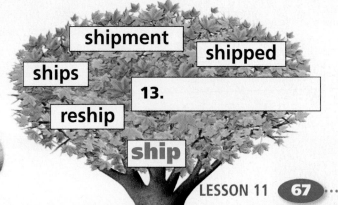

shipment

shipped

ships

13.

reship

ship

Use each spelling word once to complete the selection.

# A Life in the Circus

A circus is an exciting thing to see. Some people spend much of their life at a circus. These people work in the circus. A circus has many _____ for people to do.
1

Some circus workers train lions and tigers. They practice with these big _____ every day. They teach the
2
lions to shake _____ with their paw.
3

Some people sew things for the circus. They make pretty _____ for
4
the women to wear in the circus parade. They sew jingling _____
5
on the clown costumes.

The job of some circus workers is to drive the circus _____ from town to town. Sometimes a
6
circus must go to another country. Some of the workers must sail on _____.
7
Others fly in _____.
8
Circuses also have women and _____ who don't
9
travel at all. These people sit at _____ in offices.
10
One of their jobs is to plan where the circus will go next.

Circus people work hard, but they have fun, too. Circus cooks make sure that everyone has a good breakfast. Sometimes clowns do a special juggling act when the cooks' _____ are turned. On those
11
mornings the circus cooks serve scrambled _____!
12

men
dresses
eggs
ships
vans
cats
hands
jobs
jets
bells
desks
backs

## Spelling and Writing

### Word List

- men
- dresses
- eggs
- ships
- vans
- cats
- hands
- jobs
- jets
- bells
- desks
- backs

### Write to the Point

Which circus job would you like? Write three or four sentences about the job. Tell what you would like about it. Try to use spelling words from this lesson in your sentences.

Use the strategies on page 7 when you are not sure how to spell a word.

### Proofreading

Proofread the e-mail below. Use proofreading marks to correct four spelling mistakes, one capitalization mistake, and one punctuation mistake.

Proofreading Marks
- ⬭ spell correctly
- ≡ capitalize
- ⊙ add period

---

**e-mail**

| Address Book | Attachment | Check Spelling | Send | Save Draft | Cancel |

James,

I went to the circus on its last day here. I watched

the workers do their jobz. I saw mens put big cats

in cages Some workers carried boxs on their

backes. They put them in vans. they're going to your

town next!

Sam

---

# Dictionary Skills

**Entry Words**  A singular word names one thing. To find a plural word in a dictionary, look for its singular form. For example, to find **cats**, look for **cat**.

> **cat**  *plural*  **cats.** A small furry animal. *Why is a **cat** a good pet? (Because it is purr-fect!)*

Write these plural words in alphabetical order. Then look each one up in the Spelling Dictionary. Write the entry word and its page number.

eggs    jets    bells

| Plural | Entry Word | Page |
|--------|-----------|------|
| 1. _____ | _____ | _____ |
| 2. _____ | _____ | _____ |
| 3. _____ | _____ | _____ |

## Challenge Yourself

What do you think each Challenge Word means? Check the Spelling Dictionary to see if you are right. Then use the Challenge Words to write sentences on separate paper.

**Challenge Words**
ducklings
batches
recesses

4. Max made three **batches** of cookies.

5. The **ducklings** swam near their mother.

6. My class gets two **recesses** every day.

# Lesson 12

# Unit 2 Review
## Lessons 7–11

Use the steps on page 6 to study words that are hard for you.

**7**
six
this
will
pick

## Words with Short **i**

Write the spelling word for each meaning.

1. to choose something _____

2. the number before seven _____

3. going to _____

4. the thing here _____

**8**
live
give
think
sister

## More Words with Short **i**

Write the spelling word for each clue.

5. what you do with a present _____

6. what a girl can be _____

7. what you do with your brain _____

8. what you do in your home _____

**9**
not
block
was
what

## Words with Short **o**

Write the spelling word that completes each sentence.

9. I put a red _____ on top of the blue one.

10. Mr. Silva _____ not at school yesterday.

**11.** Tell me _____ you want to eat.

**12.** Leo is going, but I am _____.

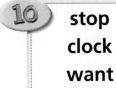

**stop**
**clock**
**want**
**wash**

## More Words with Short o

Unscramble the letters in dark type to make a spelling word. Write the word to complete the sentence.

**13. natw**   I _____ to go home now.

**14. locck**   The _____ has stopped ticking.

**15. stpo**   Please _____ the car at the corner.

**16. shwa**   I have to _____ this messy shirt.

**11**

**hands**
**desks**
**dresses**
**men**

## Plural Words

Write the spelling word that belongs in each group.

**17.** ears, _____, feet

**18.** tables, chairs, _____

**19.** women, _____, children

**20.** _____, coats, hats

## 21. Short i Words

_____

_____

_____

_____

_____

_____

_____

_____

## 22. Short o Words

_____

_____

_____

_____

_____

_____

_____

_____

# Review Sort

| what | give | want | this |
|------|------|------|------|
| six | block | stop | was |
| clock | pick | sister | will |
| think | not | wash | live |

**21.** Write the **eight** short i words.

**22.** Write the **eight** short o words. Circle the letter that spells the short o sound in each word.

Tell how these three words are alike.

**23. cats    ships    hands**

_____

_____

Tell how these three words are alike. Then tell how they are different.

**24. desks    dresses    men**

_____

_____

# Writer's Workshop

## A Narrative

A narrative is a story. Every good narrative has a beginning, a middle, and an end. Writers tell about the story characters at the beginning of a story. They also tell where the story takes place. Here is the beginning of Victor's story.

**Prewriting**  Victor used a story map to plan his story. Victor's story map is shown here. Study what Victor did.

### Sammy Grows Up

Sammy the skunk sat in the woods. His sisters were at summer camp. Sammy was too young to go to camp. He was too young for everything. He wished he could grow up! Sammy started to cry.

**Beginning**
Sammy wished he could grow up.

**Middle**
An elf heard Sammy's wish. He made Sammy a grown-up.

**End**
Sammy wished to be a little skunk again.

## It's Your Turn!

Write your own story. First, decide what to write about. Next, make a story map. Then, follow the other steps in the writing process—writing, revising, proofreading, and publishing. Try to use spelling words from this lesson in your story.

# Words with Short u

bus

## 1. u Words

_____
_____
_____
_____
_____
_____
_____
_____
_____
_____
_____
_____

## 2. o Words

_____
_____

sun
under
club
run
bug
from
mud
summer
bus
us
up
cut
of
but

## Say and Listen

Say each spelling word. Listen for the vowel sound you hear in sun.

## Think and Sort

The vowel sound in sun is called short u. All of the spelling words have the short u sound. Spell each word aloud.

Look at the letters in each word. Think about how short u is spelled. How many spellings for short u do you see?

1. Write the **twelve** spelling words that have short u spelled u.

2. Write the **two** spelling words that have short u spelled o.

Use the steps on page 6 to study words that are hard for you.

### Spelling Patterns

The short **u** sound can be spelled **u** or **o**.

| u | o |
|---|---|
| sun | from |

## Spelling and Meaning

**Antonyms**   Antonyms are words that have opposite meanings. Write the spelling word that is an antonym of each underlined word.

1. climb <u>down</u> the pole                    _____

2. <u>over</u> the trees                    _____

3. a letter <u>to</u> you                    _____

4. gave <u>them</u> a gift                    _____

5. <u>winter</u> days                    _____

6. everyone <u>including</u> me                    _____

7. <u>walk</u> to the store                    _____

**Hink Pinks**   Hink pinks are funny pairs of rhyming words. Read each clue. Write the spelling word that completes each hink pink.

8. a big thing that Gus drives                    Gus _____

9. what you can have on a sunny day         _____ fun

10. a place to get your hair trimmed            _____ hut

11. what a baby bear uses for golf               cub _____

12. a mat made for ants and beetles            _____ rug

13. a baby rose made of dirt and water       _____ bud

**W**ord Story   One spelling word comes from the Old English word **aef**. **Aef** meant "away from." Today the spelling word means "made from." Write the word.

14. _____

**Family Tree: sun**   Think about how the **sun** words are alike in spelling and meaning. Then add another **sun** word to the tree.

suns

sunless

15.

sunning

sun

Use each spelling word once to complete the selection.

# Day Camp– What Fun!

When school lets out for

_____ , some boys and
           1

girls go to a day camp.  Day campers go

home at night.  That's why their camp is called a day camp!

Families can choose _____ many day camps.
                                          2

Weeks before summer begins, many newspapers are full

_____ ads for day camps.  The ads say things like,
           3

"Come camp with _____ .  You can ride our
                              4

_____ to and from camp."
           5

What do children do at a day camp? Each camp is different,

_____ a few things are usually the same.  Campers
           6

spend time outside in the warm summer _____ .
                                                          7

They play outdoor games and _____ races.  They
                                            8

also hike _____ and down hills or along trails.
              9

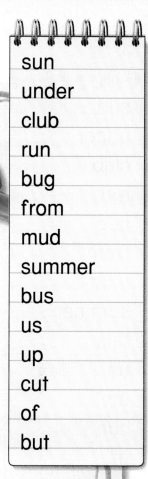

On hikes, campers study plants, animals, and other things they see.  They have fun watching a squirrel make a nest or a

_____ crawling across a leaf.  Some
          10

camps give swimming lessons.  Campers can learn how to dive and to swim _____ water.
                                               11

What do campers do when it rains, and the ground is covered with _____?  They
                                12

have fun indoors!  Campers play board games.  They may also have a craft time.  During craft time, they

paint, _____, and paste.  Some day
          13

camps have a computer _____ for the
                                14

campers, too.

Go to a day camp! You can make new friends. You are sure to have a great time, too!

sun
under
club
run
bug
from
mud
summer
bus
us
up
cut
of
but

sun
under
club
run
bug
from
mud
summer
bus
us
up
cut
of
but

### Write to the Point

Write an ad for a summer camp. Tell things that will make children want to go there. Try to use spelling words from this lesson in your ad.

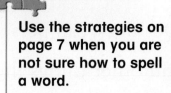

Use the strategies on page 7 when you are not sure how to spell a word.

### Proofreading

Proofread the ad below. Use proofreading marks to correct four spelling mistakes, one capitalization mistake, and one punctuation mistake.

Proofreading Marks
◯ spell correctly
≡ capitalize
⊙ add period

## Come to Camp Beans!

You can hike upp a hill and catch a buge.

you can sit in the sunn or read undr a tree

You can even swim and fish in Beans Lake.

Join us for the summer!

Call (101) 001-1010

or visit our Web site at

www.campbeans.com.

## Language Connection

**Action Words**   Some words in a sentence tell what someone does or did. These words are called action words.

| hop | skips | talked | sat |

Complete each sentence with an action word from one of the boxes.

1. I _____ races with my brother.

2. My mother _____ my hair.

3. How high can you _____?

4. Please _____ the door.

5. The mole _____ a hole.

## Challenge Yourself

What do you think each Challenge Word means? Check the Spelling Dictionary to see if you are right. Then use the Challenge Words to write sentences on separate paper.

**Challenge Words**

numb
adjust
buckle

6. Walking in the snow made my feet **numb**.

7. Please **adjust** the sound on your radio.

8. **Buckle** your seat belt before the car starts.

# More Words with Short u

skunk

**1. u Words**

_____
_____
_____
_____
_____
_____
_____
_____

**2. o Words**

_____
_____
_____
_____
_____
_____

| just |
| brother |
| jump |
| such |
| come |
| love |
| skunk |
| much |
| truck |
| mother |
| lunch |
| one |
| other |
| fun |

## Say and Listen

Say each spelling word. Listen for the short u sound.

## Think and Sort

All of the spelling words have the short u sound. Spell each word aloud.

Look at the letters in each word. Think about how short u is spelled.

1. Write the **eight** spelling words that have short u spelled u.

2. Write the **six** spelling words that have short u spelled o. Circle the three words that have a silent e at the end.

Use the steps on page 6 to study words that are hard for you.

### Spelling Patterns

The short u sound can be spelled u or o.

| u | o |
|---|---|
| just | come |

## Spelling and Meaning

**Word Meanings**  Write the spelling word for each meaning.
Use the Spelling Dictionary if you need to.

1. a good time _____
2. a lot _____
3. exactly _____
4. very _____
5. to like a lot _____
6. different _____

**Partner Words**  Complete each sentence.
Write the spelling word that goes with the underlined word.

7. The cats <u>go</u> out in the morning and _____ in at night.

8. A rabbit can <u>hop</u>. A frog can _____.

9. The girl is a <u>sister</u>. The boy is a _____.

10. A <u>father</u> is a man. A _____ is a woman.

11. We eat _____ at noon and <u>dinner</u> at six.

12. I have _____ nose and <u>two</u> eyes.

13. Will we ride in a _____ or fly in a <u>plane</u>?

**W**ord Story  Native Americans call one animal a **segonku**. The settlers couldn't say the Native American name. It has black and white fur and a bushy tail. Write the spelling word that names the animal.

14. _____

**Family Tree: jump**  Think about how the **jump** words are alike in spelling and meaning. Then add another **jump** word to the tree.

jumped

jumps

jumpy

15. _____

jump

Use each spelling word once to complete the story.

# A Pet of Our Own

Mom had tried to grow a vegetable garden for years. It was

_____ harder than you might think. That was
<sub>1</sub>

because of our neighbor, Mr. Bonzo. He had rabbits. Those

rabbits made _____ a mess in our garden! They ate
<sub>2</sub>

the peas and _____ vegetables for _____.
<sub>3</sub> <sub>4</sub>

They would leap and _____ on the lettuce. They
<sub>5</sub>

slept on the string beans.

Sometimes my _____ tried to talk to Mr. Bonzo
<sub>6</sub>

about his rabbits. He said, "I _____ to watch my
<sub>7</sub>

rabbits play in your garden. It must make you happy to see them

having _____."
<sub>8</sub>

Rabbits having fun in

her garden did not make

Mom a bit happy. "I

_____ don't
<sub>9</sub>

know what to do,"

she said. Then

_____ day
<sub>10</sub>

she got an idea.

"You kids _____ with me," she said to
                    11
us.  "It's time you had a pet of your own."  We hopped

in the _____ and headed for town.
         12

My younger _____, Sammy, and I were
                      13
excited.  "May we get a dog?" I asked.

"We need something fiercer than a dog," said Mom.

"A tiger?" asked Sammy.

"No, smaller than a tiger," said Mom.

"A snake?" I asked in a brave voice.

"No, I don't like snakes," said Mom.

We bought the best pet that the store had.  And

now we never have any rabbits in our garden.  What

did we come home with?  We got a _____!
                                            14

just
brother
jump
such
come
love
skunk
much
truck
mother
lunch
one
other
fun

### Write to the Point

Think about the story "A Pet of Our Own." Pretend you are the person who tells the story. Then write a letter to Mr. Bonzo. Tell him about the new pet in your garden. Try to use spelling words from this lesson in your letter.

Use the strategies on page 7 when you are not sure how to spell a word.

### Proofreading

Proofread the e-mail below. Use proofreading marks to correct four spelling mistakes, one capitalization mistake, and one punctuation mistake.

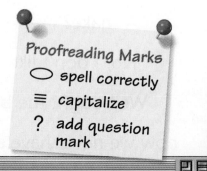

Proofreading Marks
◯ spell correctly
≡ capitalize
? add question mark

just
brother
jump
such
come
love
skunk
much
truck
mother
lunch
one
other
fun

**e-mail**

| Address Book | Attachment | Check Spelling | Send | Save Draft | Cancel |

Ben,

We got a skunk! My muther and i put him in

our garden. He is fun to watch. Mom jist came

home in the truk. It is time for lonch. Will you

come over and see our skunk

this afternoon

Theo

# Language Connection

**Exclamation Points**  Use an exclamation point at the end of a sentence that shows strong feeling or surprise.

> My frog won a blue ribbon**!**

The words in each sentence below are out of order. Put the words in order and write the sentence correctly. Remember to put an exclamation point at the end.

**1.** are fun Frog contests

_____

**2.** at has my brother frog Look the

_____

**3.** can jump high very That frog

_____

**4.** feet It jump more can ten than

_____

# Challenge Yourself

What do you think each Challenge Word means? Check the Spelling Dictionary to see if you are right. Then use the Challenge Words to write sentences on separate paper.

| Challenge Words |
| :---: |
| insult |
| blush |
| sponge |

**5.** It's an **insult** to call someone a skunk.

**6.** I began to **blush** when I saw the gum in my hair.

**7.** Wash the sink with a **sponge**.

# Words with Long a

whale

## 1. a-consonant-e Words

_____
_____
_____
_____
_____
_____
_____
_____

## 2. ay Words

_____
_____
_____
_____
_____

## 3. a Word

_____

game
baby
today
came
play
bake
whale
ate
name
say
brave
stay
maybe
gave

## Say and Listen

Say each spelling word. Listen for the vowel sound you hear in game.

## Think and Sort

The vowel sound in game is called long a. All of the spelling words have the long a sound. Spell each word aloud.

Look at the letters in each word. Think about how long a is spelled.

1. Write the **eight** words with long a spelled a-consonant-e.

2. Write the **five** words with long a spelled ay.

3. Write the **one** word with long a spelled a.

Use the steps on page 6 to study words that are hard for you.

## Spelling Patterns

The long a sound can be spelled a-consonant-e, ay, or a.

| a-consonant-e | ay | a |
|---|---|---|
| game | stay | baby |

**Synonyms**  Synonyms are words that have the same meaning. Write the spelling word that is a synonym for each word below.

1. cook  _____

2. fearless  _____

3. speak  _____

4. perhaps  _____

5. wait  _____

**Word Meanings**  Write the spelling word for each meaning. Use the Spelling Dictionary if you need to.

6. to have fun  _____

7. this day  _____

8. contest played with rules  _____

9. handed over  _____

10. what a person or thing is called  _____

11. swallowed food  _____

12. a young child  _____

13. moved towards  _____

**W**ord Story   Long ago English sailors called one animal a **hwael**. It is the biggest sea animal of all. Write the spelling that we use today to name this animal.

14. _____

**Family Tree: play**  Think about how the **play** words are alike in spelling and meaning. Then add another **play** word to the tree.

replay

played

15.

playful

play

Use each spelling word once to complete the story.

## Sports

# Alex Tate's Big Day

_____ was a very special day for Alex Tate
         1
and his fans.  It was his birthday.  He was playing in a very

exciting football _____.  The stands were packed
                        2
with people shouting out his _____.  Alex's fans
                                    3
could not _____ in their seats.
                 4
    Alex was ready to _____ when the game
                              5
began.  Right away he raced to a touchdown for the Colts.

He ended the game with a touchdown, too.  The rest of his

team _____ a loud cheer.  This _____
          6                                              7
player had won the game on his birthday!

game
baby
today
came
play
bake
whale
ate
name
say
brave
stay
maybe
gave

Three cooks had taken the time to _____
8
a cake as big as a _____. At the end of the
9
game, the fans _____ onto the field.
10
Everyone sang to Alex.  They all _____
11
a piece of the big cake.

The other boys on Alex's team _____
12
that he thinks about football all the time.  "I've loved
the game ever since I was a _____," says
13
Alex. _____ his love for the game is what
14
makes him so good!

## Write to the Point

Write a story about a game you have played or have been to see. Use spelling words from this lesson in your story.

## Proofreading

Proofread the diary page below. Use proofreading marks to correct four spelling mistakes, one capitalization mistake, and one punctuation mistake.

Use the strategies on page 7 when you are not sure how to spell a word.

Proofreading Marks
- ◯ spell correctly
- ≡ capitalize
- ⊙ add period

### Word List
- game
- baby
- today
- came
- play
- bake
- whale
- ate
- name
- say
- brave
- stay
- maybe
- gave

December 12

Dear Diary,

Alex tate cam to my home.  We ate

snacks.  Then we talked about the gaem.

Alex said that the best pley was at the

end Then he gave me a football with his

name on it. I can't wait to show it to

Jake. Todae was a great day!

# Dictionary Skills

**ABC Order**  The words in a dictionary are in ABC order. Many words begin with the same letter, so the second letter is used to put them in ABC order.

Look at the two words below. Both words begin with **b**. The second letter must be used to put the words in ABC order. The letter **a** comes before **r**, so **bag** comes before **break**.

| b**a**g | b**r**eak |
| --- | --- |

Write the following words in alphabetical order.

bake     brave     blame     big     box     bed

1. _____

2. _____

3. _____

4. _____

5. _____

6. _____

## Challenge Yourself

Write the Challenge Word for each clue. Check the Spelling Dictionary to see if you are right. Then use separate paper to write sentences. Show that you understand the meaning of each Challenge Word.

**Challenge Words**

delay

bacon

fade

7. Many people eat this with eggs and toast.  _____

8. Jeans do this after many washings.  _____

9. If you put something off until later, you do this.  _____

# More Words with Long a

train

**1. ai Words**

_____
_____
_____
_____
_____
_____
_____
_____
_____
_____
_____
_____

**2. ei Word**

_____

**3. ey Word**

_____

chain
gain
eight
tail
paint
nail
pail
they
snail
rain
wait
mail
train
sail

## Say and Listen

Say each spelling word. Listen for the long a sound.

## Think and Sort

All of the spelling words have the long a sound. Spell each word aloud.

Look at the letters in each word. Think about how long a is spelled. How many spellings for long a do you see?

1. Write the **twelve** spelling words that have long a spelled ai.

2. Write the **one** spelling word that has long a spelled ei.

3. Write the **one** spelling word that has long a spelled ey.

Use the steps on page 6 to study words that are hard for you.

### Spelling Patterns

The long a sound can be spelled ai, ei, or ey.

| ai | ei | ey |
|---|---|---|
| pail | eight | they |

## Spelling and Meaning

**Word Groups**   Write the spelling word that belongs in each group.

1. wind, snow, _____
2. boat, plane, _____
3. hammer, saw, _____
4. grow, add, _____
5. draw, color, _____
6. turtle, worm, _____
7. he, she, _____
8. leash, rope, _____

**Homophones**   Homophones are words that sound the same but have different spellings and meanings. Complete each sentence by writing the spelling word that is a homophone for the underlined word.

9. The _____ for your boat is on <u>sale</u>.

10. He turned <u>pale</u> when he dropped the _____.

11. Jesse <u>ate</u> breakfast at _____.

12. I had to _____ for him to lift the <u>weight</u>.

13. The <u>tale</u> was about a cat with a long _____.

**W**ord Story   In France long ago, a bag used to carry letters was called a **male**. One spelling word sounds the same but is spelled differently. It means "letters and packages." Write the word.

14. _____

**Family Tree: paint**   Think about how the **paint** words are alike in spelling and meaning. Then add another **paint** word to the tree.

painted

painter

repaint

15.

paint

Use each spelling word once to complete the poem.

# The Letter

What would you do if you saw a long tail

Sticking out of a letter you got in the _____?
<br>1

Would you yell, "This thing belongs in a _____!"?
<br>2

Would you feed it a worm or maybe a _____?
<br>3

Would you jump in a boat and put up a _____?
<br>4

Would you chew a finger and bite a _____?
<br>5

Would you _____ a sign that said, "For Sale"?
<br>6

If you called the police because you started to worry,

Do you think _____ would come in a hurry?
<br>7

Would you take the thing out and twist it

Into the shape of an _____,
<br>8

Or would you leave it alone and look at it

And wait and wait and _____?
<br>9

Would you wrap it in paper that's plain?

Would you send it away on a _____?
10

Would you leave it outside in the _____?
11

Would you tie it all up with a _____?
12

Would you wonder how many pounds it could

_____?
13

I know what I'd do if I saw a long _____
14

Sticking out of a letter I got in the mail.

I'd open the letter, and then with a shout

I'd say, "Hi, there, Dragon! It's time to come out!"

chain
gain
eight
tail
paint
nail
pail
they
snail
rain
wait
mail
train
sail

chain
gain
eight
tail
paint
nail
pail
they
snail
rain
wait
mail
train
sail

## Write to the Point

Make up a funny animal. It might be a dog with wings or a snail that talks! Write a story about your animal. Try to use spelling words from this lesson in your story.

**Use the strategies on page 7 when you are not sure how to spell a word.**

## Proofreading

Proofread the letter below. Use proofreading marks to correct four spelling mistakes, one capitalization mistake, and one punctuation mistake.

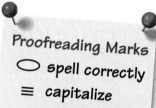

Proofreading Marks
◯ spell correctly
≡ capitalize
? add question mark

625 Oak Street

Columbus, OH 43216

June 10, 2003

Dear Andrew,

I can't waite until you come to see me! are you

going to take the trane  I am getting a pet snale in

eighte days. I will let you hold it.

Your friend,

Malik

## Dictionary Skills

**More Than One Meaning** Some words have more than one meaning. Read the entry for **paint** from the Spelling Dictionary. **Paint** has two meanings. Each meaning has a number in front of it.

> **paint 1.** *plural* **paints.** Something to color with. *We bought blue **paint** for the walls in my room.* **2.** To cover something with paint. *Please don't **paint** our front porch and steps purple!*
> **painted, painting**

Write **1** or **2** to tell which meaning of **paint** is used in each sentence.

1. My father will paint my room yellow. _____

2. We bought the paint for my room yesterday. _____

3. I spilled paint on the rug. _____

4. Will you help me paint the fence? _____

5. Do you want to draw or paint? _____

## Challenge Yourself

What do you think each Challenge Word means? Check the Spelling Dictionary to see if you are right. Then use the Challenge Words to write sentences on separate paper.

| Challenge Words |
| --- |
| bravery |
| dainty |
| faithful |

6. It took **bravery** to jump off the high diving board.

7. The dress was covered with **dainty** flowers.

8. A **faithful** pet will never run away from home.

# Words with ed or ing

fishing

**1. ed Words**

_____
_____
_____
_____
_____

**2. ing Words**

_____
_____
_____
_____
_____
_____

helping
tricked
wishing
ended
fishing
wished
dressing
picking
handed
thanked
thinking
asked
fished
catching

## Say and Listen

Say the spelling words. Listen for the ending sounds.

## Think and Sort

A **base word** is a word that can be used to make other words.

Each spelling word is made of a base word and the ending ed or ing.

Look at each word. Think about the base word and the ending. Spell each word aloud.

1. Write the **seven** spelling words that end in ed.

2. Write the **seven** spelling words that end in ing.

Use the steps on page 6 to study words that are hard for you.

## Spelling Patterns

The endings **ed** and **ing** can be added to base words to make new words.

fish + ed = fished | fish + ing = fishing

**Antonyms**  Antonyms are words that have opposite meanings. Write the spelling word that is an antonym of each word below.

1. answered  _____
2. began  _____
3. hurting  _____
4. throwing  _____

**Clues**  Write the spelling word for each clue.

5. what you did if you caught some fish  _____
6. what you did if you were polite  _____
7. what you did when you hoped  _____
8. sitting with bait at the end of a pole  _____
9. taking an apple from a tree  _____
10. putting clothes on  _____
11. what someone did to play a joke on you  _____
12. what you are doing if you are hoping  _____
13. using your brain  _____

**W**ord Story  One spelling word comes from the very old word **capere**. **Capere** meant "to get hold of." All the letters except the first two have changed. Write the spelling word that means "getting hold of."

14. _____

**Family Tree: thinking**  Thinking is a form of **think**. Think about how the **think** words are alike in spelling and meaning. Then add another **think** word to the tree.

thinking    rethink

15.

thinker

think

Use each spelling word once to complete the story.

# Rabbit and Turtle

Rabbit spent most of his time teasing Turtle. He teased Turtle for walking slowly. Turtle _____ he could run as fast
<sub>1</sub>

as Rabbit. One day Turtle was

_____ he could beat
<sub>2</sub>

Rabbit in a race. He wrote a note and

_____ it to Rabbit.
<sub>3</sub>

> Meet me under the oak tree for a race to the river. Owl will be the judge.

Rabbit got all dressed up for the race. He put on his new purple running shoes and a bright headband. He spent quite a long time _____ himself. Turtle just wore his shell.
<sub>4</sub>

The race began at noon. Rabbit dashed past Turtle. Soon he was far ahead. He stopped and began _____ berries.
<sub>5</sub>

Then he saw a pond and went _____. He sat and
<sub>6</sub>

_____ for a long time. He did not know that Turtle was
<sub>7</sub>

slowly _____ up with him.
<sub>8</sub>

Soon Turtle passed Rabbit. But Turtle was so quiet that Rabbit never saw him. Turtle kept slowly walking. At last he saw the river and the finish line.

When Turtle crossed the finish line, Owl said that the race had _____9_____. She gave Turtle a blue ribbon, and Turtle _____10_____ her politely.

A minute later Rabbit came running by, holding the five fish he had caught. He _____11_____ Owl for his blue ribbon. Then he saw that Turtle had the ribbon. "How could you win? You must have _____12_____ me! Did you have friends _____13_____ you?"

"No," said Turtle. "I had my own four feet. And I just kept _____14_____ that slow but sure wins the race!"

helping
tricked
wishing
ended
fishing
wished
dressing
picking
handed
thanked
thinking
asked
fished
catching

| |
|---|
| helping |
| tricked |
| wishing |
| ended |
| fishing |
| wished |
| dressing |
| picking |
| handed |
| thanked |
| thinking |
| asked |
| fished |
| catching |

## Write to the Point

Write a paragraph about Rabbit and Turtle's race. Tell why the slower animal was able to win. Tell what you think the rabbit learned. Try to use spelling words from this lesson in your paragraph.

Use the strategies on page 7 when you are not sure how to spell a word.

## Proofreading

Proofread the paragraph below. Use proofreading marks to correct four spelling mistakes, one capitalization mistake, and one punctuation mistake.

Proofreading Marks
◯ spell correctly
≡ capitalize
⊙ add period

The race ended, and Turtle won.

He thankd Owl for the ribbon Rabbit felt

triked. he wishd that he had won. Rabbit

was not very smart. He should not have

gone fisheng.

## Language Connection

**Present and Past Tenses**   Words that end with ed tell about the past. Words that end with ing tell about now or something that keeps going on. Write the word from the boxes that completes each sentence.

**1.** I _____ Pam rake leaves when it started to rain.

**2.** I like _____ Pam, but not in the rain!

**3.** Yesterday I _____ for directions to Jim's party.

**4.** I got lost on the way, so I kept _____ for directions.

**5.** My brother _____ me into doing his chores.

**6.** Everyone was _____ me on April Fool's Day.

## ⭐ Challenge Yourself

What do you think each Challenge Word means? Check the Spelling Dictionary to see if you are right. Then use the Challenge Words to write sentences on separate paper.

| Challenge Words |
| --- |
| **denying** |
| **claimed** |
| **alerting** |

**7.** My friend **claimed** she saw a purple cow.

**8.** Diego kept **denying** that he had eaten the cookies.

**9.** The alarm is **alerting** the police.

## Lesson 18

# Unit 3 Review
## Lessons 13–17

Use the steps on page 6 to study words that are hard for you.

**13**

cut
under
from
of

## Words with Short **u**

Write the spelling word that completes each sentence and rhymes with the underlined word.

1. The <u>thunder</u> sent little Jim

   _____ the bed.

2. Victoria and I <u>love</u> the color

   _____ the sky.

3. It is hard to _____ a <u>nut</u>.

4. The <u>hum</u> came _____ my room.

**14**

much
just
other
come

## More Words with Short **u**

Unscramble the letters in dark type to make a spelling word. Write the word to complete the sentence.

5. **emoc**  Will Grandmother _____ to the party?

6. **sjut**  This book is _____ what I wanted.

7. **umhc**  We ate too _____ popcorn at the movie.

8. **tehor**  Mom liked the _____ shirt more than this one.

## 15 Words with Long **a**

**gave**
**maybe**
**say**
**baby**

Write the spelling word that goes with the underlined word or words.

9. A <u>mother</u> is big. A _____ is small.

10. We <u>sing</u> songs. We _____ words.

11. Tim <u>handed</u> me a frog. I _____ it right back.

12. Mom and Dad didn't say <u>yes</u> or <u>no</u>. They said _____.

## 16 More Words with Long **a**

**train**
**wait**
**eight**
**they**

Write the spelling word that completes each sentence.

13. My dog had _____ puppies.

14. The _____ was an hour late.

15. I will _____ for you after school.

16. Are _____ your brothers?

## 17 Words with **ed** or **ing**

**asked**
**thanked**
**helping**
**thinking**

Write the spelling word for each meaning.

17. using the mind _____

18. questioned someone _____

19. said that you were grateful _____

20. doing something useful _____

**21. Short u Spelled u**

_____

_____

_____

_____

**22. Short u Spelled o**

_____

_____

_____

**23. Long a Spelled a-consonant-e**

_____

**24. Long a Spelled ay**

_____

_____

**25. Long a Spelled ai**

_____

_____

## Review Sort

| cut | say | maybe | train |
| gave | just | other | from |
| come | much | under | wait |

**21.** Write the **four** words that have short u spelled u.

**22.** Write the **three** words that have short u spelled o.

**23.** Write the **one** word that has long a spelled a-consonant-e.

**24.** Write the **two** words that have long a spelled ay.

**25.** Write the **two** words that have long a spelled ai.

These four words have been sorted into two groups. Tell how the words in each group are alike.

**26.** thinking     helping

_____

_____

**27.** asked     thanked

_____

_____

# Writer's Workshop

## A Friendly Letter

People write to their friends for many reasons. They write to share feelings or to tell news about their lives. Sometimes they write to invite their friends to a party. Here is part of Kara's letter to Ramon.

7160 Elm Street
Oak City, TX 75428
November 2, 2003

Dear Ramon,

Next Saturday is my birthday. I'm going to be eight years old. Mom said I can invite some friends to a party. I hope you can come! The party begins at 2:00 P.M. at my house.

**Prewriting** Kara followed the steps in the writing process to write her letter. First she made a list of things to say in her letter. This way, she would not leave out any important facts. Part of Kara's list is shown here. Study what Kara did.

Party for my birthday
Saturday, 2:00 to 4:00 P.M.
my address
bring bathing suit
my phone number

## It's Your Turn!

Get ready to write your own letter. First decide to whom you will write. Make a list of things to say in your letter. Then follow the other steps in the writing process—writing, revising, proofreading, and publishing. Try to use spelling words from this lesson in your letter.

# Words with Long e

feet

**1. e Words**

_____
_____
_____
_____

**2. ee Words**

_____
_____
_____
_____
_____
_____
_____
_____

**3. e-consonant-e Word**

_____

**4. eo Word**

_____

| |
|---|
| we |
| people |
| see |
| green |
| she |
| he |
| keep |
| feet |
| these |
| bees |
| street |
| week |
| being |
| three |

## Say and Listen

Say each spelling word. Listen for the vowel sound you hear in we.

## Think and Sort

The vowel sound in we is called long e. All of the spelling words have the long e sound. Spell each word aloud.

1. Write the **four** words with long e spelled e.

2. Write the **eight** words with long e spelled ee.

3. Write the **one** word with long e spelled e-consonant-e.

4. Write the **one** word with long e spelled eo.

Use the steps on page 6 to study words that are hard for you.

## Spelling Patterns

The long e sound can be spelled e, ee, e-consonant-e, or eo.

| e | ee | e-consonant-e | eo |
|---|---|---|---|
| we | keep | these | people |

## Spelling and Meaning

**Word Groups**  Write the spelling word that belongs in each group.

1. ants, wasps, _____
2. yellow, _____, red
3. legs, _____, toes
4. _____, him, his
5. day, _____, month
6. _____, her, hers
7. them, those, _____
8. _____, us, our

**Synonyms**  Synonyms are words that have the same meaning. Write the spelling word that is a synonym for each word below.

9. look      _____
10. persons  _____
11. road     _____
12. acting   _____
13. save     _____

**W**ord Story  One of the spelling words is the name for a number. It is written **drei** in German, **trois** in French, and **tres** in Spanish. Long ago the word was spelled **thre**. Write the word.

14. _____

**Family Tree: see**  Think about how the **see** words are alike in spelling and meaning. Then add another **see** word to the tree.

sees

saw

15. spew

seen

see

unseen

Use each spelling word once to complete the story.

# Grandfather's Race

Kevin and Abby went to _____ a bicycle race.
                                                    1
The race was more than _____ miles long.  Many
                                   2
_____ came to watch the race.  Police stood near
        3
the _____.  Their job was to _____
              4                                          5
people away from the racers.

The bicycles came around the corner.  A rider in a bright

_____ shirt was in front.  "Hey!  That's your
        6
grandfather!" yelled Kevin.  "I've never seen him go so fast.

How does _____ do it?"
                    7

"By pedaling his _____ really fast!"
                              8
Abby said. "He's also riding a racing bike. On our
bikes, _____ could never go that fast."
              9
After the race, Abby ran to her grandfather. "You
won!" _____ shouted happily. Then she
             10
saw the _____.
              11

Her grandfather jumped around and ducked
his head. "Ouch!" he yelled. "Well, I wasn't
_____ very careful," he told Abby.
         12
"I bumped into a beehive. Out came the bees.
I didn't know how fast I could ride until I tried
to race _____ bees. I won't be able to
            13
touch my neck for a _____. Let's get
                              14
out of here! I beat all the other racers, but I lost
the race with the bees!"

we
people
see
green
she
he
keep
feet
these
bees
street
week
being
three

| |
|---|
| we |
| people |
| see |
| green |
| she |
| he |
| keep |
| feet |
| these |
| bees |
| street |
| week |
| being |
| three |

## Write to the Point

Pretend you are Abby. Write a letter to a friend. Tell how your grandfather won the race. Try to use spelling words from this lesson in your letter.

Use the strategies on page 7 when you are not sure how to spell a word.

## Proofreading

Proofread the newspaper story below. Use proofreading marks to correct four spelling mistakes, one capitalization mistake, and one punctuation mistake.

Proofreading Marks
◯ spell correctly
≡ capitalize
⊙ add period

### Sports Buzz

## Redtown Runners Take a Swim

Early Friday morning the peopel of Redtown stood along the streete by the park. They waited for the runners to pass by them. soon they saw the runners jumping around and waving their hands. Some beez were chasing them! The runners jumped in the pond to kep from being stung The race was over!

## Language Connection

**Capital Letters**   Use a capital letter to begin the names of cities and states.

| | |
|---|---|
| **D**enver | **M**iami |
| **C**olorado | **F**lorida |

The sentences below have mistakes in capital letters and spelling. Write each sentence correctly.

1. I have been to ohio threa times.

   _____

2. My grandfather is in dallas this weke.

   _____

3. Theez trees grow all over maine.

   _____

4. We went to se my aunt in seattle.

   _____

## ⭐ Challenge Yourself

What do you think each Challenge Word means? Check the Spelling Dictionary to see if you are right. Then use the Challenge Words to write sentences on separate paper.

| Challenge Words |
|---|
| athlete |
| freeze |
| belief |

5. The best **athlete** was given a blue ribbon.

6. The ponds here **freeze** every winter.

7. My **belief** is that stealing is wrong.

# More Words with Long e

**1. ea Words**

_____
_____
_____
_____
_____
_____
_____
_____

**2. y Words**

_____
_____
_____
_____
_____
_____

happy
clean
very
please
leap
funny
peach
eat
city
heat
puppy
dream
penny
mean

## Say and Listen

Say each spelling word. Listen for the long e sound.

## Think and Sort

All of the spelling words have the long e sound. Spell each word aloud.

Look at the letters in each word. Think about how long e is spelled. How many spellings for long e do you see?

1. Write the **eight** spelling words that have long e spelled ea.

2. Write the **six** spelling words that have long e spelled y.

Use the steps on page 6 to study words that are hard for you.

**Spelling Patterns**

The long e sound can be spelled ea or y.

| ea | y |
|----|----|
| eat | happy |

## Spelling and Meaning

**Antonyms**   Antonyms are words that have opposite meanings. Write the spelling word that is an antonym of the word in dark type.

1. The clown made us feel _____.   **sad**

2. Please wear a _____ shirt.   **dirty**

3. Do not be _____ to animals.   **kind**

4. You can _____ this in the oven.   **cool**

**Clues**   Write the spelling word for each clue.

5. This place has many people and buildings.   _____

6. Say this to ask for something.   _____

7. This fruit has a fuzzy skin.   _____

8. Frogs do this to move.   _____

9. Use this word instead of **silly**.   _____

10. People do this to food.   _____

11. Every big dog was once this.   _____

12. This coin is worth one cent.   _____

13. When you are asleep, you do this.   _____

**W**ord Story   Many English words come from Latin. Latin was the language spoken in Rome long ago. One spelling word comes from the Latin word **verus**. It meant "truly" or "really." Write the spelling word.

14. _____

**Family Tree: clean**   Think about how the **clean** words are alike in spelling and meaning. Then add another **clean** word to the tree.

cleaning

cleaner

15.

cleanly

unclean

clean

Use each spelling word once to complete the story.

# Lucky Penny

It was a hot summer day in the _____.
                                    1

A _____ and a dime lay on the sidewalk.  They
        2

were hoping someone would pick them up.  The dime was

becoming very grouchy because of the _____.
                                          3

"No one's ever going to pick you up," it said to the penny.

   "Don't be so _____ to me," said the penny.
                    4

"I might make someone _____ someday."
                            5

   "No one wants a penny these days," snapped the dime.

"You can't buy an apple or a _____ with a
                                  6

penny.  You can't buy anything to _____ with a
                                        7

penny.  You can't buy a pet with a penny, either," the dime

went on.  "You can't buy a kitten or a _____ or a
                                            8

goldfish."

   The dime was making the penny feel sad.  "Some days I

_____ about being a new penny," it said.  "I'm dirty
      9

and old now.  Once I was shiny and _____."
                                        10

Just then a boy came by and stopped.  The penny got a _____ feeling.  The little boy was squeezing the penny in his hand.  "Here's an old one!" he cried.  "May I _____ keep it, Grandma?"

His grandmother said, "This is a _____ old penny, Ruben.  It would be a very good one to collect."

The penny felt its heart _____ for joy. Ruben put the penny in his pocket and gave the dime to his grandmother.

"Good-bye, dime," the penny sang out. "Do you see?  I do make someone happy!"

| happy |
| clean |
| very |
| please |
| leap |
| funny |
| peach |
| eat |
| city |
| heat |
| puppy |
| dream |
| penny |
| mean |

## Spelling and Writing

happy
clean
very
please
leap
funny
peach
eat
city
heat
puppy
dream
penny
mean

### Write to the Point

Ruben found an old penny. Think about something you have found or would like to find. Write a paragraph about it. Try to use spelling words from this lesson.

**Use the strategies on page 7 when you are not sure how to spell a word.**

### Proofreading

Proofread the letter below. Use proofreading marks to correct four spelling mistakes, one capitalization mistake, and one punctuation mistake.

Proofreading Marks
⬭ spell correctly
≡ capitalize
⊙ add period

233 Park Lane

peru, IL 61354

April 12, 2003

Dear John,

I found a verry old peny last week I made it bright and cleen. I am going to take it to a coin show in the citty. Will you go with me?

Your friend,

Anton

# Dictionary Skills

**Guide Words**   Every dictionary page has two guide words at the top. The first guide word is the first entry word on the page. The second guide word is the last entry word on the page.

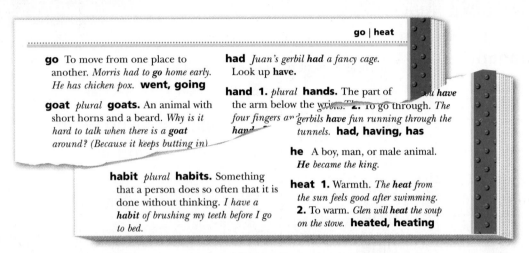

Write these entry words in alphabetical order. Then look up each one in the Spelling Dictionary. Write the guide words for the word.

happy          eat          leap

**Entry Word**                                    **Guide Words**

1. _____    _____    _____

2. _____    _____    _____

3. _____    _____    _____

## Challenge Yourself

Use the Spelling Dictionary to answer these questions. Then use the Challenge Words to write sentences on separate paper.

**Challenge Words**

disease

cheap

cheat

4. Can a net catch a **disease?** _____

5. Is a meal **cheap** if it costs fifty cents? _____

6. Can a person **cheat** on a lamp? _____

# Words with Long i

bike

**1. i-consonant-e Words**

_____

_____

_____

_____

_____

_____

_____

_____

_____

_____

_____

_____

**2. i Word**

_____

**3. eye Word**

_____

like
find
ice
bike
side
nine
write
mine
ride
white
eye
hide
inside
five

## Say and Listen

Say each spelling word. Listen for the vowel sound you hear in like.

## Think and Sort

The vowel sound in like is called long i. All of the spelling words have the long i sound. Spell each word aloud.

Look at the letters in each word. Think about how long i is spelled.

1. Write the **twelve** words with long i spelled i-consonant-e.

2. Write the **one** word with long i spelled i.

3. Write the **one** word with long i spelled eye.

Use the steps on page 6 to study words that are hard for you.

### Spelling Patterns

The long **i** sound can be spelled **i-consonant-e**, **i**, or **eye**.

| i-consonant-e | i | eye |
|---|---|---|
| ride | find | eye |

**Word Meanings**   Write the spelling word for each meaning. Use the Spelling Dictionary if you need to.

1. something with wheels to ride on _____

2. to enjoy _____

3. to sit on and be carried _____

4. the lightest color _____

5. to make words with a pencil _____

6. into _____

**Rhymes**   Write the spelling word that completes each sentence and rhymes with the underlined word.

7. Let's _____ out how to <u>wind</u> the clock.

8. Did you <u>try</u> to blink your left _____?

9. Did the cat _____ under the <u>slide</u>?

10. We planted all _____ of the <u>pine</u> trees.

11. The left _____ of the road is <u>wide</u>.

12. I slipped <u>twice</u> on the snow and _____.

13. Her soup is cold, but _____ is <u>fine</u>.

**W**ord Story   Long ago English people used the word **fimfi** to name the number after four. The word later became **fif**. Write the spelling we use now.

14. _____

**Family Tree: white**   Think about how the **white** words are alike in spelling and meaning. Then add another **white** word to the tree.

whiten

whiter

15.

whitener

white

Use each spelling word once to complete the diary entry.

# Arctic Explorer

December 8

Dear Diary,

    Today I want to _____ about the Arctic.  An
                   1

uncle of _____ lived in the Arctic from 1990 to 1999.
           2

That's _____ whole years!  He said there was snow
       3

as far as the _____ could see.
          4

    I would _____ to explore the Arctic.  All that
          5

snow and _____ would be beautiful to see.  I could
       6

_____ a dog sled across it.  That would be more
    7

fun than riding my _____!  I would look for animals
          8

that _____ from other animals in the snow.
     9

I would build a snow house and live in it, too.
I could look out and see miles of _____
                                              10
snow.  If I found a little animal that was hurt, I could
bring it _____ the house.  I would take
              11
care of it.

It would be fun to spend _____ or six
                                        12
years going all over the Arctic.  I would ride from
one _____ to the other.  Maybe I would
          13
_____ one little place that no one else
      14
has discovered.  Then I would be famous.

My uncle said that he will take me to the Arctic if
he ever goes again.  We could explore it together.
I hope he decides to go soon!

like
find
ice
bike
side
nine
write
mine
ride
white
eye
hide
inside
five

like
find
ice
bike
side
nine
write
mine
ride
white
eye
hide
inside
five

## Write to the Point

Pretend you are an explorer. You can go anywhere in the world. Write a paragraph. Tell where you want to go and why. Try to use spelling words from this lesson in your paragraph.

**Use the strategies on page 7 when you are not sure how to spell a word.**

## Proofreading

Proofread the e-mail below. Use proofreading marks to correct four spelling mistakes, one capitalization mistake, and one punctuation mistake.

**Proofreading Marks**
◯ spell correctly
≡ capitalize
⊙ add period

**e-mail**

| Address Book | Attachment | Check Spelling | Send | Save Draft | Cancel |

Hi, Allie!

I really liek Alaska. Today we rode a sled over

the ise. a team of wite dogs pulled us. We rode for

five miles Then we went insid our cabin and lit a

fire. Write and tell me how your new

kitten is doing. What's her name?

Meg

## Language Connection

**Present and Past Tenses**  Some words show action happening now, or in the present. Some words show action in the past. Look at the chart below. Notice the different spellings.

| Present | Past |
|---------|-------|
| do | did |
| find | found |
| ride | rode |

Choose the correct word in dark type to complete each sentence. Write the word on the line.

1. Watch my kittens (**hide**, **hid**) under my bed.  _____

2. They (**hide**, **hid**) there last night, too.  _____

3. Dad (**write**, **wrote**) a silly story for us.  _____

4. We can (**write**, **wrote**) a poem about him.  _____

5. Do you (**like**, **liked**) to ice skate?  _____

6. Mom (**like**, **liked**) the present we gave her.  _____

## Challenge Yourself

Write the Challenge Word for each clue. Check the Spelling Dictionary to see if you are right. Then use the Challenge Words to write sentences on separate paper.

**Challenge Words**
license
climate
advice

7. You might give this to a friend.  _____

8. You need one to drive a car.  _____

9. The North Pole has a cold one. The desert has a hot one.  _____

# More Words with Long i

tiger

## Word List

1. **i Words**

_____
_____
_____

2. **y Words**

_____
_____
_____
_____
_____
_____
_____

3. **ie Words**

_____
_____
_____

4. **igh Word**

_____

sky
pie
tiny
cry
lion
tie
why
by
try
tiger
high
lie
my
fly

## Say and Listen

Say each spelling word. Listen for the long i sound.

## Think and Sort

All of the spelling words have the long i sound. Spell each word aloud.

Look at the letters in each word. Think about how long i is spelled.

1. Write the **three** spelling words with long i spelled i.

2. Write the **seven** spelling words with long i spelled y.

3. Write the **three** spelling words with long i spelled ie.

4. Write the **one** spelling word with long i spelled igh.

Use the steps on page 6 to study words that are hard for you.

### Spelling Patterns

The long i sound can be spelled i, y, ie, or igh.

| i | y | ie | igh |
|---|---|----|-----|
| tiny | sky | lie | high |

## Spelling and Meaning

**Antonyms**  Antonyms are words that have opposite meanings. Write the spelling word that is an antonym of each underlined word.

1. The cat climbed to the <u>low</u> branch.  _____

2. Don't <u>laugh</u> over spilled milk.  _____

3. Look at that <u>large</u> mouse!  _____

4. He was sorry he told the <u>truth</u>.  _____

5. This is <u>your</u> hat.  _____

**What's Missing?**  Write the missing spelling words.

6. eat _____ and ice cream

7. wear a shirt and _____

8. the mane on the _____

9. _____ and try again

10. don't know _____

11. clouds in the _____

12. stripes on the _____

13. sit _____ him

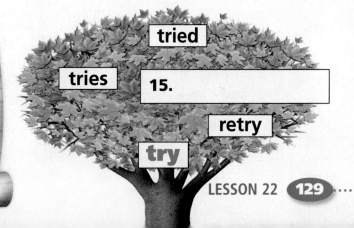

W**ord Story**   How would you like to **fliugan**? That's an Old German word. In Old English it was **fleogan**. The word tells what birds and airplanes do. Write the spelling word as it is spelled today.

14. _____

**Family Tree: try**  Think about how the **try** words are alike in spelling and meaning. Then add another **try** word to the tree.

tried

tries

15.

retry

try

Use each spelling word once to complete the story.

# Cloud Watching

On windy spring days, I like to _____ on my back and watch the clouds in the _____. Clouds used to look like big white puffs to me. I _____ to look at them carefully now. I see some real surprises!

The sky today has lots of clouds. One of them has stripes like a _____. I watch a bird _____ past it. Watch out, bird! Above me is a horse with a long tail. The tail begins to curl. I watch it _____ itself into a knot.

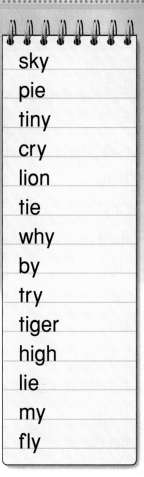

sky
pie
tiny
cry
lion
tie
why
by
try
tiger
high
lie
my
fly

A cloud way up _____ is a very tasty
                    7
surprise.  It's an apple _____.  It looks
                           8
like it is missing a _____ little bite.
                        9
Maybe that mouse cloud sailed _____
                                 10
it and nibbled on it.

Above the school are two _____
                            11
cubs.  Their mouths are open.  I think they are
starting to _____ for the mother lion.
              12
I never feel like crying while I'm watching clouds.
I could spend _____ whole day looking
                 13
at them.  Do you see _____
                        14
it is so much fun?

sky
pie
tiny
cry
lion
tie
why
by
try
tiger
high
lie
my
fly

## Write to the Point

In "Cloud Watching" the writer tells what he likes to do on spring days. Write a few sentences telling things that you like to do on spring days. Try to use spelling words from this lesson in your sentences.

Use the strategies on page 7 when you are not sure how to spell a word.

## Proofreading

Proofread the journal page below. Use proofreading marks to correct four spelling mistakes, one capitalization mistake, and one punctuation mistake.

Proofreading Marks
⬯ spell correctly
≡ capitalize
⊙ add period

march 3

Today the skye was very blue. The clouds

were big and fluffy. I drew a tiger on

some paper and made a kite with it. I

wanted the kite to touch a cloud. It

looked tinee in the air, but it did not flie

high enough I will trie again next week.

Maybe then my kite will touch a cloud.

## Dictionary Skills

**More Than One Meaning** Some words have more than one meaning. Study the Spelling Dictionary entry for **tie**. Then write the number of the meaning that best fits each sentence below.

> **tie 1.** *plural* **ties.** A necktie. *He spilled something on his* **tie**. **2.** An equal score. *The pie-eating contest ended in a* **tie**. **3.** To attach something with string or rope. *She tried to* **tie** *Mei's shoelaces together.* **tied, tying**

**Meaning**

1. Will you please **tie** my shoelaces for me? _____

2. The frog-jumping contest ended in a **tie**. _____

3. Dad should wear a **tie** to Robin's party. _____

4. **Tie** this rope around the tree trunk. _____

5. The man's **tie** matched his shirt. _____

## Challenge Yourself

What do you think each Challenge Word means? Check the Spelling Dictionary to see if you are right. Then use the Challenge Words to write sentences on separate paper.

**Challenge Words**

tying
rhyme
diet

6. Amy is **tying** her shoelaces.

7. I like to write poems that **rhyme**.

8. Some animals can live on a **diet** of fish.

# Lesson 23

# More Words with ed or ing

jogging

### 1. ed Words

_____
_____
_____
_____
_____
_____
_____

### 2. ing Words

_____
_____
_____
_____
_____
_____
_____

dropping
cutting
dropped
spotted
stopping
hopped
jogged
jogging
running
shopped
hopping
stopped
dotted
shopping

## Say and Listen

Say the spelling words. Listen for the ending sounds.

## Think and Sort

Each spelling word is made by adding ed or ing to a base word. Each base word ends with a short vowel and consonant.

Look at the letters in each spelling word. Think about how the base word changes when ed or ing is added. Spell each word aloud.

1. Write the **seven** spelling words that end in ed.

2. Write the **seven** spelling words that end in ing.

Use the steps on page 6 to study words that are hard for you.

### Spelling Patterns

Some base words end with a short vowel and a consonant. The final consonant is usually doubled when **ed** or **ing** is added.

hop + ed = hopped | hop + ing = hopping

## Spelling and Meaning

**Word Meanings**  Write the spelling word for each meaning.

1. moved up and down quickly  _____

2. moving at a slow, steady trot  _____

3. marked with a round point  _____

4. ended  _____

5. looked for things to buy  _____

6. let something fall  _____

**Synonyms**  Synonyms are words that have the same meaning. Write the spelling word that is a synonym for each word in dark type.

7. The apples are _____ off the tree.  **falling**

8. The woman _____ around the block.  **trotted**

9. We saw that the rain was _____.  **ending**

10. The children are _____ on one foot.  **jumping**

11. We saw a man _____ to his car.  **racing**

12. The spilled paint _____ the floor.  **marked**

13. Mom is _____ for some new shoes.  **looking**

**W**ord Story  In Iceland long ago, **kuti** meant "knife." In Old English the word became **cutten** and meant "to cut." One of the spelling words comes from **kuti** and **cutten**. Write the word.

14. _____

**Family Tree: spotted**  Spotted is a form of **spot**. Think about how the **spot** words are alike in spelling and meaning. Then add another **spot** word to the tree.

spotless

spots

15.

spotted

spot

Use each spelling word once to complete the poem.

# Stop Benny's Hops!

Benny was hopping and _____.
<sub>1</sub>

He hopped and hopped without _____!
<sub>2</sub>

His friends liked his trick

And watched him hop on his stick

For an hour and half without _____.
<sub>3</sub>


Benny said running was not fun.

"If you run, you're just like everyone.

When I'm hopping, I'm soaring!

I think _____ is boring,"
<sub>4</sub>

Said Benny while eating a bun.


His family went _____ with Benny.
<sub>5</sub>

His mother said, "Benny looks silly.

He has hopped and _____.
<sub>6</sub>

Every time that we've _____.
<sub>7</sub>

He will never stop, will he?"

Benny knocked over plants that were potted

And the living room rug became _____8_____.

"Benny, hop outdoors,

Not on these floors.

With mud our rug is all _____9_____!"


Benny's father didn't know what to do

With a son like a strange kangaroo.

"It's time that he _____10_____!

I want that pogo stick _____11_____,

Or else he'll soon live at the zoo!"


Benny's pogo stick rests on the floor.

"I'm afraid I can't hop anymore.

I'm _____12_____ the hopping short,

I'll go _____13_____ for sport."

And he happily _____14_____ out the door.

dropping
cutting
dropped
spotted
stopping
hopped
jogged
jogging
running
shopped
hopping
stopped
dotted
shopping

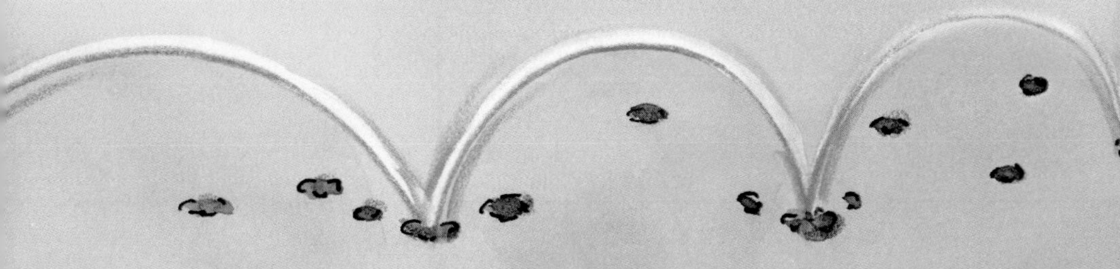

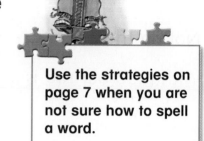

**dropping**
**cutting**
**dropped**
**spotted**
**stopping**
**hopped**
**jogged**
**jogging**
**running**
**shopped**
**hopping**
**stopped**
**dotted**
**shopping**

## Write to the Point

Benny liked to hop and jog. Write a poem about what you like to do for exercise. Try to use spelling words from this lesson.

Use the strategies on page 7 when you are not sure how to spell a word.

## Proofreading

Proofread the postcard below. Use proofreading marks to correct four spelling mistakes, one capitalization mistake, and one punctuation mistake.

Proofreading Marks
◯ spell correctly
≡ capitalize
? add question mark

Dear Juan,

I went joging today along the

beach. I jogd for a long time. there

was no stopin me. Everyone stopped

to wave at me as I went runnig by.

What are you doing for fun

Your friend,

Hector

Juan Bravo

7601 Water Road

Houston, TX 77035

## Language Connection

**Verb Forms**   Some words show action. These words are called verbs, and they have different forms. Look at the box below. Notice the different forms of the verb.

> Dad likes to **jog** every day.
> Mom **jogged** with him last week.
> Scooter is **jogging** with him today.

Choose the correct verb in dark type to complete each sentence. Write the word on the line.

1. Maria will be (**shop**, **shopping**) in town.  _____

2. I (**shop**, **shopped**) for shoes last week.  _____

3. Nathan was (**hop**, **hopping**) like a rabbit.  _____

4. His pet frog (**hop**, **hopped**) right out of its bowl!  _____

5. Dad (**stop**, **stopped**) the car at the light.  _____

6. The bus is (**stop**, **stopping**) at every corner.  _____

## Challenge Yourself

What do you think each Challenge Word means? Check the Spelling Dictionary to see if you are right. Then use the Challenge Words to write sentences on separate paper.

**Challenge Words**

admitting
strutting
propped

7. **Admitting** a mistake is hard.

8. The rooster was **strutting** around the barnyard.

9. I **propped** my bat against the fence.

# Unit 4 Review
## Lessons 19–23

Use the steps on page 6 to study words that are hard for you.

**19**
being
street
week
people

## Words with Long e

Write the spelling word that completes each sentence.

1. I like _____ with my grandfather.

2. Our vacation starts in a _____.

3. A lot of cars were on the _____.

4. My dad invited fifty _____ to his party.

**20**
clean
please
very
funny

## More Words with Long e

Write the spelling word for each meaning.

5. not dirty          _____

6. really             _____

7. silly              _____

8. be so kind as to   _____

**21**
write
white
find
eye

## Words with Long i

Write the spelling word that belongs in each group.

9. read, _____, count

10. ear, nose, _____

11. see, look, _____

12. black, _____, gray

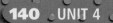

**22**

tiny
why
tie
high

## More Words with Long **i**

Write the spelling word for each clue.

**13.** A man wears this around his neck.

_____

**14.** This word means "very small."

_____

**15.** Use this word to ask for a reason.

_____

**16.** This word is the opposite of **low**.

_____

**23**

dropped
stopped
running
hopping

## More Words with **ed** or **ing**

Write the spelling word that completes each sentence.

**17.** The rabbit was _____ across our lawn.

**18.** The rain _____ in time for our picnic.

**19.** I _____ all the dishes on the floor!

**20.** Ling is _____ to catch up with us.

**21. Long e Words**

_____

_____

_____

_____

_____

_____

_____

_____

**22. Long i Words**

_____

_____

_____

_____

_____

_____

_____

# Review Sort

| white | write | eye | please |
| street | very | clean | being |
| tie | week | why | high |
| funny | find | people | |

**21.** Write the **eight** long e words. Circle the letters that spell long e in each word.

**22.** Write the **seven** long i words. Circle the letters that spell long i in each word.

These four words have been sorted into two groups. Tell how the words in each group are alike.

**23. stopped     dropped**

_____

_____

**24. hopping     running**

_____

_____

# Writer's Workshop

## A Description

A description tells about someone or something. The writer uses words that help the reader see, hear, smell, taste, and feel what is being described. Read Nina's description.

**Prewriting**   To write her description, Nina followed the steps in the writing process. She began with a senses web. She wrote down all of the things about the tree house that she could see and touch. Part of Nina's senses web is shown here. Study what she did.

### My Tree House

My tree house has four walls made of wood. The roof is flat and also made of wood. The outside is painted dark brown. The walls inside are green. One wall has a small hole for a window and a big hole for a door.

### My Tree House

**See**
wood walls
flat roof made of wood
brown outside
green inside
small hole for window
big hole for door

## It's Your Turn!

Write your own description. It can be about any special place or person in your life. Begin by making a senses web. Then follow the other steps in the writing process—writing, revising, proofreading, and publishing. Try to use spelling words from this lesson in your description.

# Words with Long o

nose

## 1. o Words

_____

_____

## 2. o-consonant-e Words

_____

_____

_____

_____

_____

_____

## 3. ow Words

_____

_____

_____

_____

go
yellow
home
rope
grow
know
no
nose
hope
stone
snow
so
hole
joke

## Say and Listen

Say each spelling word. Listen for the vowel sound you hear in go.

## Think and Sort

The vowel sound in all of the spelling words is called long o. Spell each word aloud.

Look at the letters in each word. Think about how long o is spelled.

1. Write the **three** spelling words with long o spelled o.

2. Write the **seven** spelling words with long o spelled o-consonant-e.

3. Write the **four** spelling words with long o spelled ow.

Use the steps on page 6 to study words that are hard for you.

## Spelling Patterns

The long o sound can be spelled o, o-consonant-e, or ow.

| o | o-consonant-e | ow |
|---|---|---|
| go | hole | snow |

## Spelling and Meaning

**Word Groups**  Write the spelling word that belongs in each group.

1. rain, _____, ice

2. red, blue, _____

3. eye, ear, _____

4. yes, _____, maybe

5. string, yarn, _____

**Rhymes**  Write the spelling word that completes each sentence and rhymes with the underlined word.

6. I left my brush and <u>comb</u> at _____.

7. The tiny <u>mole</u> ran down a _____.

8. I _____ you like the fancy <u>soap</u>.

9. The dinosaur <u>bone</u> turned to _____.

10. Ned <u>woke</u> me up to tell me a _____.

11. Corn plants will _____ in each <u>row</u>.

12. The <u>bow</u> was _____ big that it hid the package.

13. I cannot _____ skating with a sore <u>toe</u>.

**W**ord Story  One spelling word was once spelled **cnowen**. The word meant "to recognize." Today the word begins with a silent letter. Write the word.

14. _____

**Family Tree: hope**  Think about how the **hope** words are alike in spelling and meaning. Then add another **hope** word to the tree.

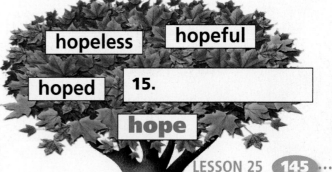

hopeless    hopeful

hoped    15.

hope

Use each spelling word once to complete the story.

# Jump Rope Rose

Rose's leg was in a cast. It all started when she went _____ skiing.
1

She put on her new ski hat. When she started to _____ down a
2

tall hill, the ski hat slid down to her _____ and covered her
3

eyes. She couldn't see the deep _____ in the trail.
4

Rose fell and hit her leg on a large _____. The leg
5

was broken.

At first, having a cast was fun for Rose. Her friends wrote on it. They visited her at _____ and told her funny
6

stories. Her father brought her a pot of bulbs, and she watched them _____ into pink tulips. But then spring
7

came, and everyone but Rose was playing outside and jumping _____. There was _____ way Rose
8                              9

could jump rope with a cast on.

"I _____ the doctor will take my cast off
10

today," Rose said to her mother. "I want to jump rope with my friends."

"Maybe he will," her mother replied, "but we really don't _____ for sure."
11

They went to the doctor's office. Rose stared at Dr. Bradford. He had a big cast on his foot!

"Hello, Rose," he said. "Look what I did water skiing. You are lucky. Today your cast comes off, but mine just went on!"

Rose felt sorry for Dr. Bradford. She told him a funny _____. The next day she sent him
12
a big pot of _____ tulips. She knew
13
how Dr. Bradford felt. She was _____
14
happy that her cast was off!

go
yellow
home
rope
grow
know
no
nose
hope
stone
snow
so
hole
joke

## Spelling and Writing

### Write to the Point

Rose's friends told her funny stories to cheer her up. Write a funny story you would tell Rose. Try to use spelling words from this lesson.

Use the strategies on page 7 when you are not sure how to spell a word.

### Proofreading

Proofread the letter below. Use proofreading marks to correct four spelling mistakes, one capitalization mistake, and one punctuation mistake.

Proofreading Marks
◯ spell correctly
≡ capitalize
? add question mark

1212 Rose Avenue

Rock Springs, WY 82942

January 19, 2003

Dear Ling,

Can you goe on a ski trip We can have fun. The

trails are marked with yellow rop. I hope the snowe

is deep. last year I hit a ston and broke my ski.

Your friend,

Luisa

## Language Connection

**Homophones**   Some words sound the same but have different spellings and different meanings. These words are called homophones. **Our** and **hour** are homophones.

Choose the correct homophone in dark type to complete each sentence. Write the word on the line.

1. "I ate the (**hole**, **whole**) doughnut," said Max.   _____

2. "Did you eat the (**hole**, **whole**) in the middle, too?" asked Mia.

   _____

3. Did you (**no**, **know**) that our sun is really a star?   _____

4. There is (**no**, **know**) way to count all the stars.   _____

5. "I will (**sew**, **so**) a new dress for Meg," said my mom.

   _____

6. "And (**so**, **sew**) will I," said Aunt Jane.   _____

7. "She will look (**so**, **sew**) pretty," said my mom.   _____

## ☆Challenge Yourself

Write the Challenge Word for each clue. Check the Spelling Dictionary to see if you are right. Then use the Challenge Words to write sentences on separate paper.

| Challenge Words |
| --- |
| hopeful |
| explode |
| bony |

8. A very thin horse is this.   _____

9. You are this when you want a good thing to happen.

   _____

10. Firecrackers do this on the Fourth of July.   _____

# More Words with Long o

goat

**1. o Words**

_____
_____
_____
_____
_____
_____
_____
_____
_____
_____

**2. oa Words**

_____
_____
_____
_____

cold
road
gold
goat
old
coat
sold
boat
open
over
roll
most
hold
told

## Say and Listen

Say each spelling word. Listen for the long o sound.

## Think and Sort

All of the spelling words have the long o sound. Spell each word aloud.

Look at the letters in each word. Think about how long o is spelled. How many spellings for long o do you see?

1. Write the **ten** spelling words that have long o spelled o.

2. Write the **four** spelling words that have long o spelled oa.

> Use the steps on page 6 to study words that are hard for you.

### Spelling Patterns

The long o sound can be spelled o or oa.

| o | oa |
|---|---|
| cold | goat |

## Spelling and Meaning

**Letter Scramble**  Unscramble the letters in dark type to make a spelling word. Write the word on the line.

1. **dols**  bought and _____

2. **roev**  under or _____

3. **atoc**  _____ and hat

4. **locd**  hot and _____

5. **enpo**  _____ or closed

**Clues**  Write the spelling word for each clue.

6. This travels on the water.  _____

7. This word means "did tell."  _____

8. Many rings are made of this.  _____

9. A car drives on this.  _____

10. This farm animal has horns.  _____

11. You can do this to someone's hand.  _____

12. The opposite of **new** is this.  _____

13. This word rhymes with **toast**.  _____

**W**ord Story  Long ago the word **rotula** meant "small wheel." Later the word became **rollen** and meant "to turn over and over." What word do we use today? Write the spelling word.

14. _____

**Family Tree: open**  Think about how the **open** words are alike in spelling and meaning. Then add another **open** word to the tree.

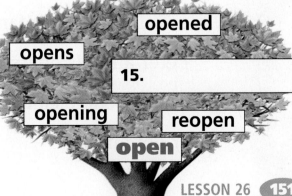

opened

opens

15.

opening

reopen

open

Use each spelling word once to complete the story.

# The Goat Boat

It was winter.  Peter and his family were hungry and _____.  They lived in a small _____
        1                                                                    2

house far out in the country.  To make money, the family _____ goat's milk to people passing by.  But this
     3

winter the narrow dirt _____ past their farm was
                                          4

closed.  The snow was much too deep.  One day Peter watched his mother _____ their last bag of beans.
                                                     5

They would soon be out of food!  Peter had to find a job in the city.  Nothing was going to _____ him back.
                                                    6

Peter called his two goats.  He took the oars out of his fishing _____.  He tied each _____ to
                         7                                      8

the boat.  He put on his _____ and packed a
                                          9

_____ to eat on the way to the city.  Then Peter
 10

_____ his family good-bye.
 11

Peter and his goats had fun as they slid _____
                                                                                     12

the hills.  People came running and asking for rides. Peter got an idea.

"Yes, you may have a ride!" he told them. "But you must pay me, because I must have money to buy food."

The people were happy to pay Peter for a ride in his snow boat. It was the _____ fun they had ever had!
13

Peter never got to the city. At the end of the day, he went home to his family with a pocket full of _____ coins. Every winter day he took people for rides. He and his family never had to worry about being hungry again.
14

cold
road
gold
goat
old
coat
sold
boat
open
over
roll
most
hold
told

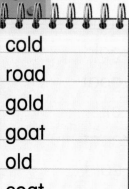

cold
road
gold
goat
old
coat
sold
boat
open
over
roll
most
hold
told

### Write to the Point

Peter sold rides on the goat boat to help his family. Write a paragraph. Tell what you have done to help somebody you know. Try to use spelling words from this lesson in your paragraph.

Use the strategies on page 7 when you are not sure how to spell a word.

### Proofreading

Proofread the ad below. Use proofreading marks to correct four spelling mistakes, one capitalization mistake, and one punctuation mistake.

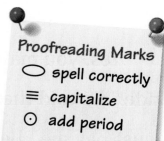

Proofreading Marks
◯ spell correctly
≡ capitalize
⊙ add period

## Goat Boat Rides!

Take a ride on a snow boat! It is the moast fun you will ever have! our brown and goeld goats will pull you in a boat. You will fly across the snow We are open six days a week. Wear a heavy cote so that you will not get coald.

# Language Connection

**Synonyms and Antonyms**   Synonyms are words that have the same meaning. Antonyms are words that have opposite meanings.

| Synonyms | Antonyms |
|---|---|
| little, small | tall, short |

Use a word from the boxes to write a synonym for each word.

**road**    **gold**    **told**    **roll**

1. street  _____
2. said  _____
3. bun  _____
4. yellow  _____

Use a word from the boxes to write an antonym for each word.

**cold**    **open**    **over**    **old**

5. under  _____
6. shut  _____
7. new  _____
8. hot  _____

## Challenge Yourself

Use the Spelling Dictionary to answer each question. Then use the Challenge Words to write sentences on separate paper.

**Challenge Words**

mold
boulder
clover

9. Can you put water in a **mold** to make ice cubes?  _____

10. Can you pick up a **boulder** with just one hand?  _____

11. Would you look for a four-leaf **clover** in a field?  _____

# The Vowel Sound in book

book

**1. oo Words**

_____

_____

_____

_____

_____

_____

_____

_____

**2. ou Words**

_____

_____

_____

**3. u Words**

_____

_____

_____

book
put
look
could
pull
would
cook
should
full
stood
cookies
good
foot
took

## Say and Listen

Say each spelling word. Listen for the vowel sound you hear in book.

## Think and Sort

All of the spelling words have the vowel sound in book. Spell each word aloud.

Look at the letters in each word. Think about how the vowel sound in book is spelled.

1. Write the **eight** spelling words that have oo.

2. Write the **three** spelling words that have ou.

3. Write the **three** spelling words that have u.

Use the steps on page 6 to study words that are hard for you.

### Spelling Patterns

The vowel sound in **book** can be spelled **oo**, **ou**, or **u**.

| oo | ou | u |
|------|-------|-----|
| book | could | put |

## Spelling and Meaning

**Word Meanings**   Write the spelling word for each meaning.

1. small, sweet cakes _____

2. a form of the word **will** _____

3. someone who makes food _____

4. to set something in place _____

5. pages fastened together _____

6. was able to do something _____

7. was upright on the feet _____

8. to have a duty _____

9. see _____

**Antonyms**   Antonyms are words that have opposite meanings. Complete each sentence by writing the spelling word that is an antonym of the word in dark type.

10. Rita will _____ your sled up the hill.   **push**

11. Mason _____ a cookie to school.   **gave**

12. The cookie jar was _____.   **empty**

13. This spaghetti tastes _____.   **bad**

**W**ord Story   One spelling word was once spelled **fot**. It named the part of the leg you stand on. The meaning has not changed, but the spelling has. Write the spelling we use today.

14. _____

**Family Tree: cook**   Think about how the **cook** words are alike in spelling and meaning. Then add another **cook** word to the tree.

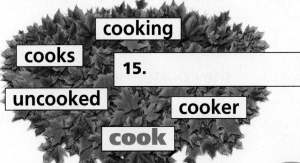

cooking

cooks

15.

uncooked

cooker

cook

Use each spelling word once to complete the story.

# The Fable of the Cookie

One day a man bought some chocolate

chip _____. He carried them
<br>1

home in a bag.  The bag broke, and two cookies fell out.

A peacock found the cookies on the grass.  "These cookies

smell so _____!  They must have been baked by a
<br>2

fine _____!" said the peacock.  He _____
<br>3  4

the cookies and hopped into a tree.

A dog was passing by.  She smelled the chocolate chip

cookies.  She _____ below the tree and said, "Please,
<br>5

dear peacock, _____ me up into the tree.  I will help
<br>6

you eat your cookies."

The peacock _____ not help the dog.  The hungry
<br>7

dog began to stamp her _____.
<br>8

A wise old cat walked by.  "Dear cat, _____ you
<br>9

help me get the cookies?" asked the dog.

"Dear peacock," purred the cat, "please _____
<br>10

the cookies down and fly away so I can _____ at your
<br>11

beautiful feathers."  But the peacock would not fly.

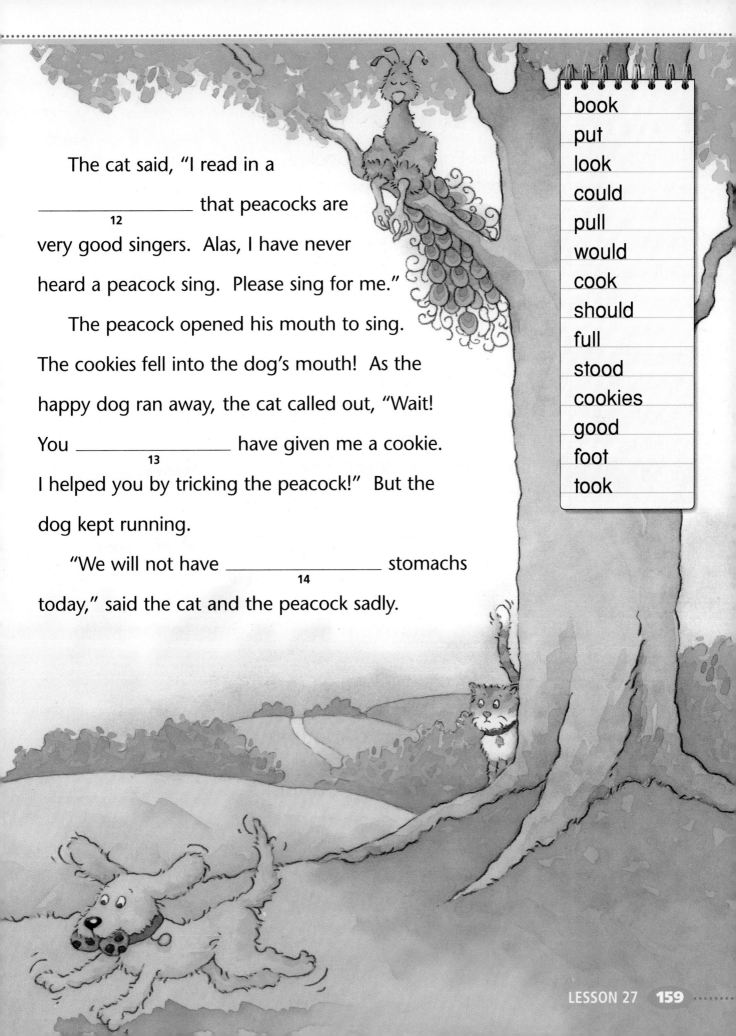

The cat said, "I read in a

_____ that peacocks are
　　　　12

very good singers.  Alas, I have never

heard a peacock sing.  Please sing for me."

　　The peacock opened his mouth to sing.

The cookies fell into the dog's mouth!  As the

happy dog ran away, the cat called out, "Wait!

You _____ have given me a cookie.
　　　13

I helped you by tricking the peacock!"  But the

dog kept running.

　　"We will not have _____ stomachs
　　　　　　　　　　　　　　14

today," said the cat and the peacock sadly.

book
put
look
could
pull
would
cook
should
full
stood
cookies
good
foot
took

book
put
look
could
pull
would
cook
should
full
stood
cookies
good
foot
took

### Write to the Point

In "The Fable of the Cookie," the cat tricked the peacock into dropping the cookies. Write sentences telling another way to get the cookies. Try to use spelling words from this lesson in your sentences.

Use the strategies on page 7 when you are not sure how to spell a word.

### Proofreading

Proofread the ad below. Use proofreading marks to correct four spelling mistakes, one capitalization mistake, and one punctuation mistake.

Proofreading Marks
◯ spell correctly
≡ capitalize
⊙ add period

**Woud you like a treat? Come to the Milk and Cookies Shop at 16 oak Street.**

**Our shop is ful of delicious cookies Take a good looke. Try some. Buy some. Our cok is the best!**

## Language Connection

**Abbreviations**   An abbreviation is a short way of writing a word. Abbreviations usually begin with a capital letter and end with a period.

> Mister = **Mr.**   Mistress = **Mrs.**
> Street = **St.**   Road = **Rd.**

The following names and addresses have mistakes. Write each one correctly.

1. mr Roy Gray _____

2. I63I Elm rd _____

3. mrs Jean Ryan _____

4. 402 Bank st. _____

5. mr. Yoshi Ono _____

6. 6800 Burnet rd. _____

7. mrs Deana Reyna _____

8. 509 State St _____

9. Mr Jackson Palmer _____

## Challenge Yourself

What do you think each Challenge Word means? Check the Spelling Dictionary to see if you are right. Then use the Challenge Words to write sentences on separate paper.

**Challenge Words**
bulletin
bushel
cookbook

10. The **bulletin** on the radio told about a bad storm.

11. A **bushel** of apples will be enough for everyone.

12. Use a **cookbook** to find out how to make bread.

# The Vowel Sound in zoo

*food*

**1. oo Words**

_____
_____
_____
_____
_____
_____

**2. ue Word**

_____

**3. ew Word**

_____

**4. o Words**

_____
_____
_____
_____

zoo
too
to
do
new
room
food
who
blue
school
tooth
soon
moon
two

## Say and Listen

Say each spelling word. Listen for the vowel sound you hear in zoo.

## Think and Sort

All of the spelling words have the vowel sound in zoo. Spell each word aloud.

Look at the letters in each spelling word. Think about how the vowel sound in zoo is spelled.

1. Write the **eight** words with oo.

2. Write the **one** word with ue.

3. Write the **one** word with ew.

4. Write the **four** words with o.

Use the steps on page 6 to study words that are hard for you.

### Spelling Patterns

The vowel sound in zoo can be spelled oo, ue, ew, or o.

| oo | ue | ew | o |
|----|----|----|----|
| zoo | blue | new | do |

## Spelling and Meaning

**Word Meanings**   Write the spelling word for each meaning.

1. a body that moves around a planet   _____
2. which person   _____
3. a place where wild animals are kept   _____
4. something to eat   _____
5. in a short time   _____
6. a hard, bony growth in the mouth   _____
7. a space in a building   _____

**Homophones**   Homophones are words that sound the same but have different spellings and meanings. Write the spelling word that completes each sentence and is a homophone of the underlined word.

8. Our _____ umbrella <u>blew</u> away.
9. The <u>two</u> boys swam _____ the shore.
10. I <u>knew</u> that Nina had a _____ puppy.
11. How many books _____ we have <u>due</u> at the library?
12. They have _____ many things <u>to</u> do.
13. Did Chad score _____ points, <u>too</u>?

**W**ord Story   Long ago the Greeks spent free time learning things. One meaning of their word **schole** was "free time." One of the spelling words comes from **schole**. Write the word.

14. _____

**Family Tree: new**   Think about how the **new** words are alike in spelling and meaning. Then add another **new** word to the tree.

newly
news
renew
15.
newest
new

Use each spelling word once to complete the selection.

# A Fish Story

Millions of years ago, a very big fish lived in the sea. It was as big as a grown-up person. It was _____ in color.
1

This big fish had six fins on its body. It used its many fins _____ swim quickly. It also had many teeth. Each _____ was very sharp. The fish used its teeth to catch its _____ and eat it. Most fish have one tail, but this fish had _____ tails.
2
3
4
5

Scientists named the fish coelacanth (SEE luh kanth). They thought it had disappeared forever, like the dinosaurs. These people were wrong!

In 1938 some men _____ were
6
fishing caught a coelacanth. They had never seen
such a strange fish. It was very big. There was
hardly enough _____ for it in the net.
7
The men did not know what they had found.

The men went to a _____ and asked
8
a teacher what the fish was. The teacher told them
that they had caught a live coelacanth. The men
had not found a _____ kind of fish.
9
They had found a very, very old one.

People _____ began looking for
10
more fish like this one. But it took 14 more years to
catch one. One night, by the light of a full
_____, another one was caught.
11
Scientists all over the world were happy to study
this fish. They all said it was _____
12
good to be true.

No _____ in the world has a
13
coelacanth. But maybe someday you can find one
in the ocean. If you _____, you could
14
become famous!

zoo
too
to
do
new
room
food
who
blue
school
tooth
soon
moon
two

zoo
too
to
do
new
room
food
who
blue
school
tooth
soon
moon
two

## Write to the Point

Draw a picture of the strangest animal you have ever seen. Then write three or four sentences telling about it. Try to use spelling words from this lesson in your sentences.

Use the strategies on page 7 when you are not sure how to spell a word.

## Proofreading

Proofread the paragraph below. Use proofreading marks to correct four spelling mistakes, one capitalization mistake, and one punctuation mistake.

Proofreading Marks
◯ spell correctly
≡ capitalize
⊙ add period

The Strange Fish

Last summer I went fishing with my

dad. I caught the strangest fish I had

ever seen. dad thought it was tew

strange to eat. I didn't know what to

doo with it. Grandpa knew the place to

call. He called the zue We soun found

out that my fish was a mudfish.

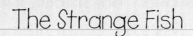

## Language Connection

**Nouns**  A noun is a word that names a person, place, or thing.

| Person | Place | Thing |
|--------|-------|-------|
| boy | city | toy |
| girl | town | dog |

Find the noun in the boxes that completes each sentence.
Then write the sentence.

room     zoo     tooth     moon

**1.** We saw lions and tigers at the ___.

_____

**2.** Chad lost a ___ at school.

_____

**3.** Which ___ should we paint next?

_____

**4.** The full ___ made the sky bright.

_____

## ☆ Challenge Yourself

Write the Challenge Word for each clue. Check the
Spelling Dictionary to see if you are right. Then
use the Challenge Words to write sentences on
separate paper.

**Challenge Words**
cocoon
bamboo
booth

**5.** This plant makes a good fishing pole.  _____

**6.** This is what a moth grows in.  _____

**7.** You can sell lemonade at one of these.  _____

# More Words with ed or ing

baking

## 1. ed Words

_____
_____
_____
_____
_____
_____

## 2. ing Words

_____
_____
_____
_____
_____
_____
_____

joking
named
baking
biked
hoped
living
liked
giving
lived
baked
riding
writing
loved
having

## Say and Listen

Say the spelling words. Listen for the ending sounds.

## Think and Sort

Each spelling word is made by adding ed or ing to a base word. Each base word ends with e.

Look at the letters in each word. Think how the base word changes when ed or ing is added. Spell each word aloud.

1. Write the **seven** spelling words that end in ed.

2. Write the **seven** spelling words that end in ing.

Use the steps on page 6 to study words that are hard for you.

### Spelling Patterns

Some base words end in silent e. The e is usually dropped before ed or ing is added to these words.

| ed | ing |
|---|---|
| like + ed = liked | joke + ing = joking |

**Word Groups**   Write the spelling word that belongs in each group.

1. hiked, skated, _____

2. reading, spelling, _____

3. frying, broiling, _____

4. laughing, teasing, _____

5. wanted, wished, _____

6. liked, cared, _____

**Synonyms**   Synonyms are words that have the same meaning. Complete each sentence by writing the spelling word that is a synonym for each word in dark type.

7. We _____ the dog Nicki.   **called**

8. We _____ a dozen cookies.   **cooked**

9. Mr. Reyna _____ in a house nearby.   **stayed**

10. We are _____ food to the birds.   **offering**

11. Are you _____ ice cream with your cake?   **getting**

12. I like _____ in the city.   **being**

13. Rosa will be _____ on a train.   **sitting**

**Word Story**   Long ago in England, **lician** meant "to please." Over time the spelling changed. The meaning became "to enjoy." Write the spelling word that comes from **lician** and means "enjoyed."

14. _____

**Family Tree: liked**  Think about how the **like** words are alike in spelling and meaning. Then add another **like** word to the tree.

likes   likable

liked   15. _____

dislike   likely

like

Use each spelling word once to complete the story.

# Mr. Banana's Inventions

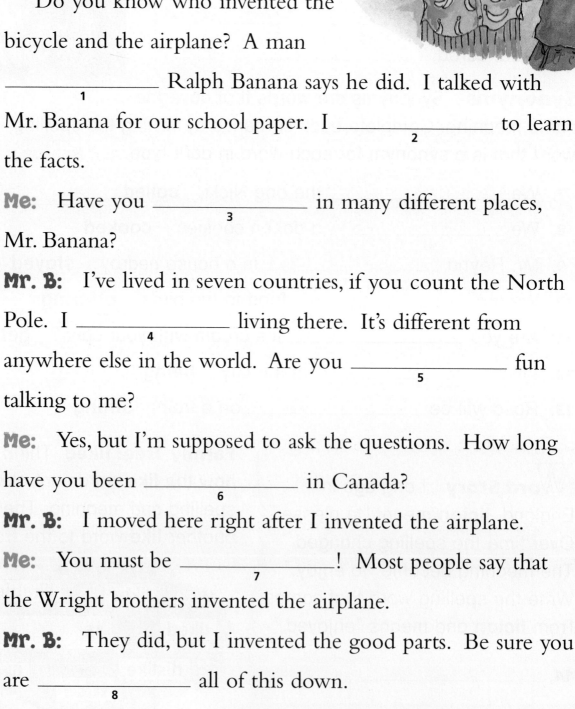

Do you know who invented the bicycle and the airplane?  A man

_____ Ralph Banana says he did.  I talked with
<sub>1</sub>

Mr. Banana for our school paper.  I _____ to learn
<sub>2</sub>

the facts.

**Me:**  Have you _____ in many different places,
<sub>3</sub>

Mr. Banana?

**Mr. B:**  I've lived in seven countries, if you count the North

Pole.  I _____ living there.  It's different from
<sub>4</sub>

anywhere else in the world.  Are you _____ fun
<sub>5</sub>

talking to me?

**Me:**  Yes, but I'm supposed to ask the questions.  How long

have you been _____ in Canada?
<sub>6</sub>

**Mr. B:**  I moved here right after I invented the airplane.

**Me:**  You must be _____!  Most people say that
<sub>7</sub>

the Wright brothers invented the airplane.

**Mr. B:**  They did, but I invented the good parts.  Be sure you

are _____ all of this down.
<sub>8</sub>

I used to be head baker at the North Pole. One day my oven blew up. When the smoke cleared, I saw something interesting.

| joking |
| named |
| baking |
| biked |
| hoped |
| living |
| liked |
| giving |
| lived |
| baked |
| riding |
| writing |
| loved |
| having |

It was as hard as metal! "My wonderful oven has _____ something I can ride," I said
9
to myself. I added two wheels and called it a bicycle. I _____ everywhere. I find
10
that riding a bicycle is much better exercise than _____ in a car. Don't you? Soon I was
11
_____ lots of bikes and _____
12                    13
them away to everyone at the North Pole.
Everyone there _____ my bicycles!
14
The next time my oven blew up, I invented the airplane. And this is a true story.

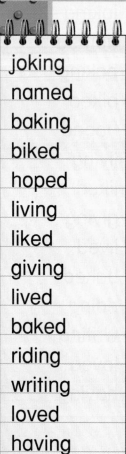

joking
named
baking
biked
hoped
living
liked
giving
lived
baked
riding
writing
loved
having

## Write to the Point

Suppose you are like Mr. Banana. What important thing could you invent? Write a paragraph telling about your invention. If you wish, give your invention a name. Try to use spelling words from this lesson in your paragraph.

Use the strategies on page 7 when you are not sure how to spell a word.

## Proofreading

Proofread the e-mail below. Use proofreading marks to correct four spelling mistakes, one capitalization mistake, and one punctuation mistake.

Proofreading Marks
⬯ spell correctly
≡ capitalize
? add question mark

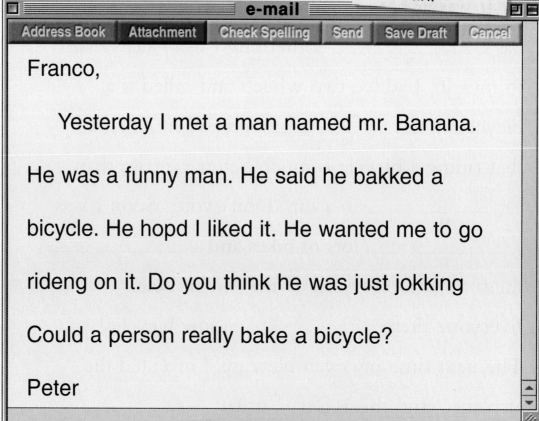

**e-mail**

Address Book | Attachment | Check Spelling | Send | Save Draft | Cancel

Franco,

Yesterday I met a man named mr. Banana.

He was a funny man. He said he bakked a

bicycle. He hopd I liked it. He wanted me to go

rideng on it. Do you think he was just jokking

Could a person really bake a bicycle?

Peter

# Dictionary Skills

**Base Words**   To find an **ed** or **ing** word in a dictionary, look for the base word entry. The **ed** and **ing** forms of a word are given as part of the base word entry.

Below are eight **ing** words. Write the base word for each one. Then look up each base word in the Spelling Dictionary and write the page number for it.

|  | **Base Word** | **Dictionary Page** |
|---|---|---|
| 1. living | _____ | _____ |
| 2. giving | _____ | _____ |
| 3. having | _____ | _____ |
| 4. writing | _____ | _____ |
| 5. loving | _____ | _____ |
| 6. biking | _____ | _____ |
| 7. naming | _____ | _____ |
| 8. liking | _____ | _____ |

## ⭐ Challenge Yourself

What do you think each Challenge Word means? Check the Spelling Dictionary to see if you are right. Then use the Challenge Words to write sentences on separate paper.

**Challenge Words**

amusing

disliked

lining

9. The clowns were **amusing** the children with funny tricks.

10. Our new kittens **disliked** getting a bath.

11. The fuzzy **lining** in my coat keeps me warm.

Use the steps on page 6 to study words that are hard for you.

**25**

no
home
know
yellow

## Words with Long o

Write the spelling word for each clue.

1. This means that you understand something. _____

2. A lemon is this color. _____

3. This is the opposite of **yes**. _____

4. The place where you live is called this. _____

**26**

cold
open
over
coat

## More Words with Long o

Write the spelling word that belongs in each group.

5. sweater, jacket, _____

6. unlock, uncover, _____

7. cool, chilly, _____

8. under, beside, _____

**27**

book
could
would
pull
put

## The Vowel Sound in **book**

Write the spelling word that completes
each sentence.

9. I enjoyed reading this _____.

10. Dan, _____ you like some soup?

11. Don't _____ the rope too hard.

12. You need to _____ your clothes away.

13. Jay, you _____ wash the dishes.

**28**

tooth
two
blue
new

## The Vowel Sound in **zoo**

Write the missing spelling word.

14. my missing _____

15. the deep _____ sea

16. one or _____ apples

17. old and _____

**29**

liked
riding
writing

## More Words with **ed** or **ing**

Write the spelling word for each meaning.

18. making words with a pencil   _____

19. enjoyed   _____

20. sitting in and being carried   _____

## 21. Words with Long o

_____

_____

_____

_____

_____

_____

## 22. Words with the Vowel Sound in book

_____

_____

_____

## 23. Words with the Vowel Sound in zoo

_____

_____

_____

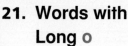

## Review Sort

| no | over | would | new |
| tooth | know | blue | open |
| cold | book | put | two |
| coat | pull | home | yellow |

**21.** Write the **eight** long o words. Circle the letter or letters that spell long o in each word.

**22.** Write the **four** words that have the vowel sound in book. Circle the letter or letters that spell the vowel sound in each word.

**23.** Write the **four** words that have the vowel sound in zoo. Circle the letter or letters that spell the vowel sound in each word.

These four words have been sorted into two groups. Tell how the words in each group are alike.

**24. liked      hoped**

_____

_____

**25. writing      riding**

_____

_____

# Writer's Workshop

## A Narrative

You know that a narrative is a story. There are many different kinds of stories. Chen liked to read stories that surprised him. He wanted to write one with a surprise ending. Here is part of Chen's story.

**Prewriting** To write his story, Chen followed the steps in the writing process. He used a story map to plan the beginning, middle, and end of his story. Study the part of Chen's story map at right.

The Surprise Guest
Theo heard the doorbell jingle. Someone had come into the restaurant. His father asked Theo to see who was there. Theo was always glad to help. He went out front. No one was there.

### Beginning
Theo heard the front doorbell. No one was there. Some food was missing.

### Middle
This happened all week. Food kept disappearing.

## It's Your Turn!

Write your own story. Pick a kind of story that you would like to read. Then follow the other steps in the writing process—writing, revising, proofreading, and publishing. Try to use spelling words from this lesson in your story.

# The Vowel Sound in out

cow

## 1. ou Words

_____
_____
_____
_____
_____
_____

## 2. ow Words

_____
_____
_____
_____
_____
_____
_____

out
found
town
sound
now
mouse
flower
round
owl
around
how
house
cow
clown

## Say and Listen

Say each spelling word. Listen for the vowel sound you hear in out.

## Think and Sort

All of the spelling words have the vowel sound in out. Spell each word aloud.

Look at the letters in each word. Think about how the vowel sound in out is spelled.

1. Write the **seven** spelling words that have ou.

2. Write the **seven** spelling words that have ow.

Use the steps on page 6 to study words that are hard for you.

## Spelling Patterns

The vowel sound in out can be spelled **ou** or **ow**.

| ou | ow |
|---|---|
| out | cow |

**Letter Scramble** Unscramble each group of letters to make a spelling word. Write the word on the line.

1. lerfow _____
2. undor _____
3. droanu _____
4. tou _____
5. nudof _____

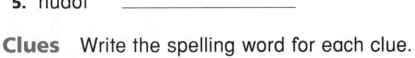

**Clues** Write the spelling word for each clue.

6. You see this person at the circus. _____
7. This is another word for **noise**. _____
8. This has a roof and a door. _____
9. Use this word to ask a question. _____
10. This bird is often called wise. _____
11. This is a small city. _____
12. A cat likes to chase this animal. _____
13. This word is the opposite of **then**. _____

**W**ord Story In Old English one spelling word was written **cu**. In other languages it was spelled **ku, ko, cae,** and **bo**. The word names an animal that moos. Write the word.

14. _____

**Family Tree: round** Think about how the **round** words are alike in spelling and meaning. Then add another **round** word to the tree.

rounded

roundest

roundness

15.

around

round

Use each spelling word once to complete the story.

# Drawing by Jill

My name is Jill. My favorite thing to do is to draw pictures. People like my pictures because they are funny. I have become a good artist.

I like to draw animals best. For me it is easy to draw a _____. I draw _____ circles to make

1                                    2

most of the mouse. I draw lines for the whiskers and tail. Right _____ I am drawing a picture of a barnyard. A

3

_____ is eating hay. A _____ is growing

4                                    5

in the ground beside the cow. I will also draw an _____

6

in a tree by the barn. I cannot hear, so I have only read about the _____ that an

7

owl makes at night. Does it really say "Whooo"?

I like drawing animals, but I know _____ 8 to draw lots of other things, too. Yesterday I drew a picture of the stores in my _____ 9 . I also drew a picture of my _____ 10 and yard. This morning I drew a picture of a circus _____ 11 . He had fallen _____ 12 of a clown car that was driving _____ 13 a tent.

I am glad that I have _____ 14 a way to share my ideas with others. Maybe when I grow up, I can draw pictures for books. Until then I will keep drawing for fun.

out
found
town
sound
now
mouse
flower
round
owl
around
how
house
cow
clown

| |
|---|
| out |
| found |
| town |
| sound |
| now |
| mouse |
| flower |
| round |
| owl |
| around |
| how |
| house |
| cow |
| clown |

## Write to the Point

Draw a picture of your town. Then write sentences telling about it. Try to use spelling words from this lesson in your sentences.

Use the strategies on page 7 when you are not sure how to spell a word.

## Proofreading

Proofread the postcard below. Use proofreading marks to correct four spelling mistakes, one capitalization mistake, and one punctuation mistake.

**Proofreading Marks**

⬯ spell correctly

≡ capitalize

? add question mark

Dear Bailey,

   I am drawing pictures of my toun. First I walked arownd to get ideas. I saw a mouse by a tree. then I fownd a big green hows. Do you like to draw Draw me a picture of your town.

                              Eric

Bailey Oakes

986 Tell Ave.

Ventura, IA

        50482

## Language Connection

**Was and Were**   The words **was** and **were** tell about the past.
**Was** tells about one person or thing. **Were** tells about two or more
persons or things.

| | | |
|---|---|---|
| I **was** | Jed **was** | the cat **was** |
| we **were** | Jed and Ted **were** | the cats **were** |

Choose the correct word in dark type to complete each sentence.
Then find the spelling mistake. Write the sentence correctly.

**1.** The dog (**was**, **were**) afraid of the sownd.

_____

**2.** The boys (**was**, **were**) glad to see the oul.

_____

**3.** The child (**was**, **were**) picking a flouer.

_____

**4.** How many stores (**was**, **were**) in that toun?

_____

**5.** A mous (**was**, **were**) hiding in my shoe.

_____

## Challenge Yourself

Write the Challenge Word for each clue. Check the
Spelling Dictionary to see if you are right. Then
use the Challenge Words to write sentences on
separate paper.

**Challenge Words**

coward

drought

brow

**6.** It is found above your eyes. _____

**7.** This is a person who is not brave. _____

**8.** A farmer does not like this. _____

# The Vowel Sound in saw

frog

## Say and Listen

Say each spelling word. Listen for the vowel sound you hear in saw.

## Think and Sort

All of the spelling words have the vowel sound in saw. Spell each word aloud.

Look at the letters in each word. Think about how the vowel sound in saw is spelled.

1. Write the **two** spelling words that have aw.

2. Write the **six** spelling words that have a.

3. Write the **six** spelling words that have o.

### Spelling words

saw
song
talk
dog
call
frog
off
ball
draw
all
lost
small
walk
long

### Word lists

1. aw Words

_____
_____

2. a Words

_____
_____
_____
_____
_____
_____

3. o Words

_____
_____
_____
_____
_____
_____

Use the steps on page 6 to study words that are hard for you.

## Spelling Patterns

The vowel sound in saw can be spelled aw, a, or o.

| aw | a | o |
|---|---|---|
| saw | ball | dog |

**Word Groups**   Write the spelling word that belongs in each group.

1. pup, hound, _____

2. yell, shout, _____

3. tadpole, toad, _____

4. run, jog, _____

5. speak, say, _____

6. paint, sketch, _____

7. looked, watched, _____

8. music, tune, _____

**Antonyms**   Antonyms are words that have opposite meanings. Complete each sentence by writing the spelling word that is an antonym of the word in dark type.

9. The room was very _____. **large**

10. Have you _____ your red hat? **found**

11. Last year her hair was _____. **short**

12. Please turn _____ the light. **on**

13. We found _____ of the missing screws. **none**

**W**ord Story   Many years ago in England, a round object used in sports was called a **beall**. The spelling of **beall** has changed only a little. Write the spelling that we use today.

14. _____

**Family Tree: call**   Think about how the **call** words are alike in spelling and meaning. Then add another **call** word to the tree.

recall

caller

15.

called

calls

call

Use each spelling word once to complete the story.

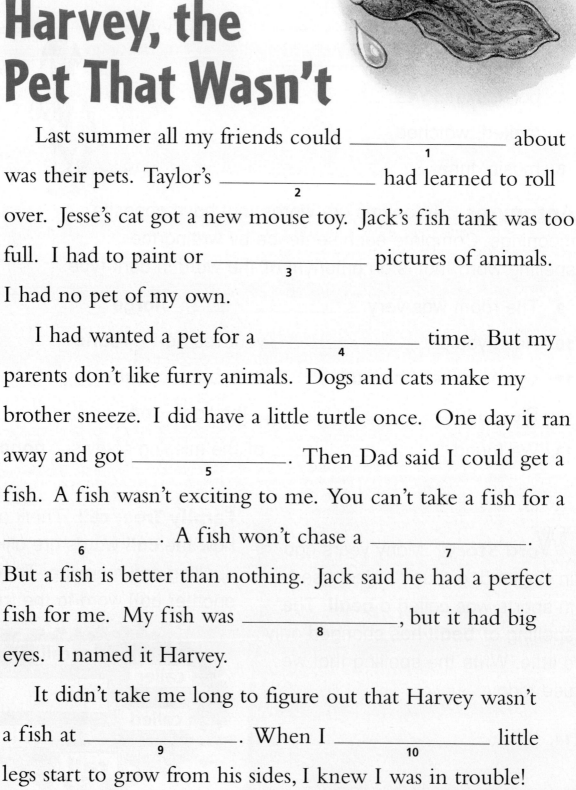

# Harvey, the Pet That Wasn't

Last summer all my friends could _____ about
        1
was their pets. Taylor's _____ had learned to roll
                2
over. Jesse's cat got a new mouse toy. Jack's fish tank was too
full. I had to paint or _____ pictures of animals.
              3
I had no pet of my own.

I had wanted a pet for a _____ time. But my
                    4
parents don't like furry animals. Dogs and cats make my
brother sneeze. I did have a little turtle once. One day it ran
away and got _____. Then Dad said I could get a
            5
fish. A fish wasn't exciting to me. You can't take a fish for a
_____. A fish won't chase a _____.
      6                                        7
But a fish is better than nothing. Jack said he had a perfect
fish for me. My fish was _____, but it had big
                      8
eyes. I named it Harvey.

It didn't take me long to figure out that Harvey wasn't
a fish at _____. When I _____ little
          9                        10
legs start to grow from his sides, I knew I was in trouble!

I could not believe my eyes. I had an about-to-be

_____ ! What would my parents say if
　　11

they saw a frog hopping down the hall? What

would happen when they heard Harvey singing

that well-known frog _____ , "Ribbit,
　　　　　　　　　　　12

Ribbit"?

　　I took my little tadpole to the pond. I watched

him swim _____ to find some friends.
　　　　　13

　　I'm not going to _____ Jack
　　　　　　　　　　　14

for a while. Not until I have thought

of a way to pay him back for his

little joke!

saw
song
talk
dog
call
frog
off
ball
draw
all
lost
small
walk
long

## Spelling and Writing

saw
song
talk
dog
call
frog
off
ball
draw
all
lost
small
walk
long

### Write to the Point

The speaker in the story wanted a pet. Write a paragraph about a pet you like. Tell why you like it. Try to use spelling words from this lesson in your paragraph.

Use the strategies on page 7 when you are not sure how to spell a word.

### Proofreading

Proofread the e-mail below. Use proofreading marks to correct four spelling mistakes, one capitalization mistake, and one punctuation mistake.

**Proofreading Marks**
◯ spell correctly
≡ capitalize
⊙ add period

**e-mail**

Address Book | Attachment | Check Spelling | Send | Save Draft | Cancel

Dear Amy,

I have a smal dog named Chip. he has longe

black hair He always comes when I cal him. Chip

loves to chase a baul. Sometimes he doesn't want

to give it back to me! Would you

like to come play catch with us?

Daniel

# Using the Spelling Table

A spelling table can help you find words in a dictionary. A spelling table shows the different spellings for sounds. Suppose you are not sure how to spell the long **e** sound in **freeze**. First, find **long e** in the spelling table. Then read the first spelling for the sound and look up **frez** in the dictionary. Look for each spelling in the dictionary until you find the correct one.

| Sound | Example Words | Spellings |
|-------|---------------|-----------|
| long e | he, eat, tree, very, people, belief | e ea ee y eo ie |

Complete each picture name by writing the correct letter or letters. Use the Spelling Table on page 213 and the Spelling Dictionary to decide on the correct letters.

1.  l_____bster

2.  athl_____

3.  cl_____ver

4.  r_____ng

5.  sp_____nge

6.  _____ite

# Challenge Yourself

Use the Spelling Dictionary to answer these questions. Then use the Challenge Words to write sentences on separate paper.

**Challenge Words**

false

haul

faucet

7. Will people trust you if you say things that are **false**? _____

8. Can a truck **haul** branches to another place? _____

9. Could you find a **faucet** in a kitchen? _____

# The Vowel Sound in for

horse

**1. o or o-consonant-e Words**

_____
_____
_____
_____
_____
_____
_____
_____
_____
_____
_____

**2. oo Words**

_____
_____

**3. ou Word**

_____

for
corn
door
or
story
short
snore
more
horse
storm
four
orange
floor
store

## Say and Listen

Say each spelling word. Listen for the vowel sound you hear in for.

## Think and Sort

All of the spelling words have the vowel sound in for. Spell each word aloud.

Look at the letters in each word. Think about how the vowel sound in for is spelled.

1. Write the **eleven** spelling words that have o or o-consonant-e.

2. Write the **two** spelling words that have oo.

3. Write the **one** spelling word that has ou.

Use the steps on page 6 to study words that are hard for you.

## Spelling Patterns

The vowel sound in for can be spelled o, o-consonant-e, oo, or ou.

| o | o-consonant-e | oo | ou |
|---|---|---|---|
| for | more | door | four |

## Spelling and Meaning

**Word Meanings** Write the spelling word for each meaning. Use the Spelling Dictionary if you need to.

1. a yellow grain _____
2. very bad weather _____
3. a place where goods are sold _____
4. not tall _____
5. the number after three _____
6. a large four-legged animal with hooves _____

**Clues** Write the spelling word for each clue.

7. You want this if you want extra. _____
8. This word is used on a gift card. _____
9. This word can join two others. _____
10. You can drink this juice for breakfast. _____
11. Some people do this when they sleep. _____
12. You go in and out through this. _____
13. People walk on this. _____

**W**ord Story One of the spelling words means "a tale." It comes from the Old French word **estorie**. In Old English it was spelled **storie**. The spelling changed over time, and **ie** became **y**. Write the spelling that we use today.

14. _____

**Family Tree: short** Think about how the **short** words are alike in spelling and meaning. Then add another **short** word to the tree.

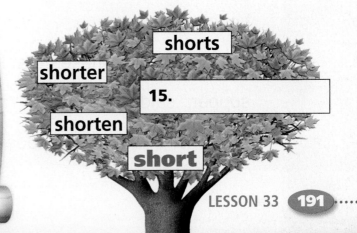

shorts

shorter

15.

shorten

short

Use each spelling word once to complete the story.

# Rainy Day Recipe

It was raining outside. "What can we do?"

Joey asked Rita. "If we had some money, we could go to

the _____."
  1

"But we don't have any money," she said. "You could tell

me a scary _____."
  2

"Oh, no! I don't know any stories. Let's go down to Uncle

Burt's until this awful _____ is over."
  3

Uncle Burt lived on the _____ just below theirs.
  4

They locked the _____ to their apartment and took
  5

the _____ elevator ride to Uncle Burt's.
  6

Uncle Burt and Scooter were in the kitchen. Scooter was a

Saint Bernard. He was almost as big as a _____!
  7

Most Saint Bernards are brown and white. Scooter was

_____ and white. Scooter was asleep. Now and
  8

then he would _____, growl, _____
  9                              10

bark in his sleep.

"I'm going to make meat loaf _____
  11

supper," said Uncle Burt. "You can read

the list of what we need, Joey."

Joey read out loud from the cookbook:

"2 pounds of hamburger

1 cup of bread crumbs

1 small can of _____
12

1 cup of grated cheese

1 chopped onion."

Uncle Burt started to cut up the onion.  The onion

made him cry.  He rubbed his eyes.  That made him

cry even _____.  He had to stop for
13

_____ or five minutes.
14

Rita put everything in a bowl.  Everyone took a turn

at mixing.  Then they put the meat loaf in the oven.

When the storm stopped, the meat loaf was ready.

"How do you like that, Scooter?"  Joey asked.

"Woof!" barked Scooter.

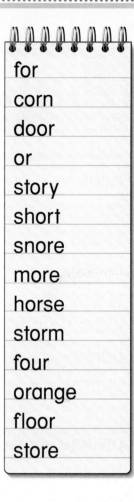

for
corn
door
or
story
short
snore
more
horse
storm
four
orange
floor
store

### Write to the Point

Do you know how to make something good to eat? Write a paragraph telling how to make the food. Try to use spelling words from this lesson in your paragraph.

| Use the strategies on page 7 when you are not sure how to spell a word. |

### Proofreading

Proofread the ad below. Use proofreading marks to correct four spelling mistakes, one capitalization mistake, and one punctuation mistake.

**Spelling words:**

for
corn
door
or
story
short
snore
more
horse
storm
four
orange
floor
store

Proofreading Marks
⬭ spell correctly
≡ capitalize
⊙ add period

## Fur and Feathers Pet Store

Feeding birds in your back yard can be fun. Our stoore has everything you need. We have cracked corne, sunflower seeds, and fruit. we also have special feeding dishes. Cut up an orenge and put it on a feeding dish In a shart time, you will have lots of feathered visitors!

## Language Connection

**End Marks**  Put a period (.) at the end of a sentence that tells something. Put a question mark (**?**) at the end of a question. Put an exclamation point (**!**) at the end of a sentence that shows strong feeling or surprise.

> It was a nice day. When did it get cold**?**
> Now we have three feet of snow**!**

Choose the correctly spelled word in dark type to complete each sentence. Then write the sentence, adding the correct end mark.

1. Snow has fallen for (**fower**, **four**) days and nights

   _____

2. Watch out for the snow above that (**door**, **dore**)

   _____

3. Do you think we will get (**more**, **mor**) snow

   _____

## Challenge Yourself

**Challenge Words**

> torch
> organ
> orchard

Use the Spelling Dictionary to answer these questions. Then use the Challenge Words to write sentences on separate paper.

4. Does a **torch** give off light?  _____

5. Could you play an **organ** while marching in a band?

   _____

6. Could you find apples in an **orchard**?  _____

# The Vowel Sound in jar

car

**1. a Word**

_____

**2. ar Words**

_____
_____
_____
_____
_____
_____
_____
_____
_____
_____
_____
_____
_____

jar
car
party
barn
arm
father
mark
farmer
star
are
dark
farm
far
art

## Say and Listen

Say each spelling word. Listen for the vowel sound you hear in jar.

## Think and Sort

All of the spelling words have the vowel sound in jar. The sound is spelled a in each word. Look at the letters in each word. Spell each word aloud.

1. Write the **one** spelling word that has a.

2. Write the **thirteen** spelling words that have ar.

Use the steps on page 6 to study words that are hard for you.

### Spelling Patterns

The vowel sound in jar can be spelled a.

| father | jar |

## Spelling and Meaning

**Word Groups**   Write the spelling word that belongs in each group.

1. gardener, rancher, _____

2. music, reading, _____

3. hand, wrist, _____

4. glass, bottle, _____

5. is, am, _____

6. garden, ranch, _____

7. brother, mother, _____

8. black, unlit, _____

**Rhymes**   Write the spelling word that completes each sentence and rhymes with the underlined word.

9. You traveled _____ in your <u>car</u>.

10. Did <u>Marty</u> go to the _____?

11. The <u>shark</u> had a _____ on its fin.

12. How <u>far</u> away is that _____?

13. The cat carried the <u>yarn</u> to the _____.

**W**ord Story   One spelling word once was a name for a wagon. Some people spelled it **carrus**. Today the spelling word is another word for **automobile**. Write the word.

14. _____

**Family Tree: farm**   Think about how the **farm** words are alike in spelling and meaning. Then add another **farm** word to the tree.

farmers   farmed

farming   15.

farmer

**farm**

Use each spelling word once to complete the story.

# The Star Party

Four children lived with their parents and grandmother on a pretty _____. The _____ and his
1                              2
wife worked hard. They had a _____ full of
3
animals to take care of every day.

One summer night the grandmother looked up at the sky. "My eyes are bad," she said sadly. "I can't see a single
_____ anymore."
4
That night after dinner, the mother and _____
5
took the children for a ride in the _____. They
6
made a plan to make the grandmother happy.

The next night the father said, "Tonight we are having a star _____. The presents _____ all ready. Let the party begin!"

The first child gave the grandmother a kitten. It had a white _____ on its face just like a star. The second child had made a bracelet of yellow stars. The grandmother put it on her _____. The third child had covered the garden with a hundred stars cut from silver paper. The garden was a work of _____.

Then the youngest child quietly handed the grandmother a glass _____ with a lid. It didn't seem to be a star present at all. He told her to open the jar outside.

The grandmother went out to the garden and took the lid off the jar. Everyone smiled. Fireflies flew all around. They glowed brightly in the _____.

"It's a jar of stars!" said the youngest child.

The grandmother said, "I love the stars you gave me. Now I don't need to see the stars that are so _____ away."

jar
car
party
barn
arm
father
mark
farmer
star
are
dark
farm
far
art

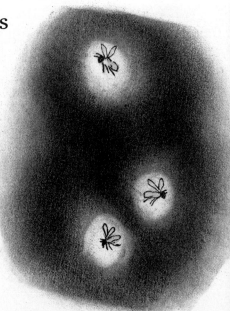

## Spelling and Writing

**Spelling words list:**

jar
car
party
barn
arm
father
mark
farmer
star
are
dark
farm
far
art

### Write to the Point

Think of another good gift for the star party. Write a paragraph that tells about the gift. Try to use spelling words from this lesson in your paragraph.

Use the strategies on page 7 when you are not sure how to spell a word.

### Proofreading

Proofread the book jacket below. Use proofreading marks to correct four spelling mistakes, one capitalization mistake, and one punctuation mistake.

**Proofreading Marks**
◯ spell correctly
≡ capitalize
? add question mark

every summer night the Clark children have a pardy when it gets daark. They chase fireflies around the barne. One night a firefly lands on a child's arem. The firefly blinks a message. What is it trying to say Read The Firefly Farm to find out.

## Dictionary Skills

**More Than One Meaning**   Some words have more than one meaning. The dictionary entries for these words give the different meanings. Study the entries below.

> **star** *plural* **stars. 1.** The sun and other bright heavenly bodies. *The* **star** *we see best at night is the North Star.* **2.** A leading actor or actress, athlete, or musician. *My brother is a super drummer. I think he will be a rock* **star**!

> **mark** *plural* **marks. 1.** A spot on something. *A wet glass will leave a* **mark** *on a table.* **2.** A grade given in school. *I got good* **marks** *on my report card.*

Use the correct word above to complete each sentence. Then write the number of the meaning used in the sentence.

1. Everyone cheered for the _____ of the show.   _____

2. Dad couldn't get the _____ off the car.   _____

3. One _____ shone brighter than the others.   _____

4. Kim got a high _____ on her art project.   _____

5. Our sun is really a _____.   _____

6. The pen left a _____ on the table.   _____

## Challenge Yourself

Write the Challenge Word for each clue. Check the Spelling Dictionary to see if you are right. Then use the Challenge Words to write sentences on separate paper.

**Challenge Words**
- barber
- depart
- harmful

7. You do this when you leave for school.   _____

8. Something that hurts you is this.   _____

9. This person cuts hair.   _____

# Lesson 35

# Words with er

painter

## Say and Listen

Say each spelling word. Listen for the ending sounds.

## Think and Sort

Each spelling word is made by adding er to a base word. In which spelling words does the spelling of the base word change?

1. **No Change to Base Word**

_____
_____
_____
_____
_____
_____
_____

2. **Final Consonant Doubled**

_____
_____
_____
_____

3. **Final e Dropped**

_____
_____
_____

colder
bigger
helper
shopper
braver
runner
writer
older
longer
jumper
flatter
faster
painter
baker

1. Write the **seven** spelling words with no change in the base word.

2. Write the **four** spelling words in which the final consonant of the base word is doubled.

3. Write the **three** spelling words in which the final e of the base word is dropped.

Use the steps on page 6 to study words that are hard for you.

## Spelling Patterns

| No Change to Base Word | Final Consonant Doubled | Final e Dropped |
|---|---|---|
| colder | flatter | braver |

**Word Meanings**   Write the spelling word for each meaning.

1. someone who shops        _____

2. someone who helps        _____

3. someone who writes stories  _____

4. more able to face danger    _____

5. someone who runs        _____

6. more flat            _____

7. someone who jumps       _____

8. one who colors things     _____

**Antonyms**   Antonyms are words that have opposite meanings. Complete each sentence by writing the spelling word that is an antonym of the word in dark type.

9. Kay is _____ than her sister.   **younger**

10. The turtle was _____ than the rabbit.   **slower**

11. My legs are _____ than yours.   **shorter**

12. Jesse's feet are _____ than mine.   **smaller**

13. The night was _____ than the day.   **hotter**

**W**ord Story   Back in the year 800, the Old English word **bacan** meant "to bake." Later, a person who baked was called a **baecere**. Write the spelling for **baecere** that we use today.

14. _____

**Family Tree: help**  Think about how the **help** words are alike in spelling and meaning. Then add another **help** word to the tree.

helpful

helps

15.

helped

helper

help

Use each spelling word once to complete the selection.

# All Kinds of Jobs

Have you thought about what job you would like to have when you grow up? You can decide when you are _____, but you can think
_____1_____
about different kinds of jobs now.

You know about many jobs around you. Would you like to work in a school? You could be a teacher or a teacher's _____. Do you like to keep up
_____2_____
with what is going on? Do you like to write stories? These are things a _____ at
_____3_____
a newspaper does. Would you like to work with food? You could be a cook or a _____.
_____4_____

Are you brave? Firefighters and police officers are _____ than many other
_____5_____
people. Maybe this kind of work is for you.

Think about the buildings you see around you. Buildings need to be built on level ground.

You could drive a bulldozer and make the ground _____ 6 than it is. Maybe you would like to make houses bright and colorful. This is what a _____ 7 does.

You can find some jobs in almost any town, even a very small town. Other jobs can be found only in _____ 8 places. Do you like to shop? Would you like to be paid for it? You might become a professional _____ 9 in a city. Professional shoppers shop and buy things for other people.

Are you a good _____ 10? Can you run _____ 11 than others? Can you run _____ 12 distances? Can you jump higher than your friends can? Would you call yourself a high _____ 13? If so, you may be able to do stunts for movies.

Maybe you would like a really different job. You could be a scientist studying the ice cap near the South Pole. You would live and work in a place that is _____ 14 than most other places. If you like peace and quiet, this job might be for you!

colder
bigger
helper
shopper
braver
runner
writer
older
longer
jumper
flatter
faster
painter
baker

## Spelling and Writing

### Write to the Point

You just read about all kinds of jobs. Think of questions you would like to ask about some of the jobs. Write two or three questions about the jobs. Try to use spelling words from this lesson in your questions.

Use the strategies on page 7 when you are not sure how to spell a word.

### Proofreading

Proofread the questions below. Use proofreading marks to correct four spelling mistakes, one capitalization mistake, and one punctuation mistake.

**Spelling Word List**

- colder
- bigger
- helper
- shopper
- braver
- runner
- writer
- older
- longer
- jumper
- flatter
- faster
- painter
- baker

Proofreading Marks
○ spell correctly
≡ capitalize
? add question mark

---

### What I Want to Know

1. Does a newspaper writter have to be a good speller?

2. What does a teacher's hepler do

3. Does a firefighter have to run fastur than most other people?

4. how early does a bakker have to get up?

# Dictionary Skills

**ABC Order**  Some of the **er** words in this lesson are describing words. To find an **er** describing word in a dictionary, look for the base word. For example, to find the word **bigger**, look for **big**.

Write these words in ABC order. Then find each word in the Spelling Dictionary. Write its page number.

colder   bigger   braver   flatter

longer   hotter   rounder

| Word | Page Number |
|------|-------------|
| **1.** _____ | _____ |
| **2.** _____ | _____ |
| **3.** _____ | _____ |
| **4.** _____ | _____ |
| **5.** _____ | _____ |
| **6.** _____ | _____ |
| **7.** _____ | _____ |

## Challenge Yourself

What do you think each Challenge Word means? Check the Spelling Dictionary to see if you are right. Then use the Challenge Words to write sentences on separate paper.

**Challenge Words**

baby sitter

beginner

dipper

8. The **baby sitter** takes care of Pedro when Mom is at work.

9. Skating is hard for a **beginner**.

10. Long ago people used a **dipper** to pour water.

# Unit 6 Review
## Lessons 31–35

Use the steps on page 6 to study words that are hard for you.

 **31** out
around
town
flower

## The Vowel Sound in **out**

Write the spelling word for each meaning.

1. the part of a plant that blooms

   _____

2. not in   _____

3. a large village   _____

4. in a circle   _____

**32** saw
talk
small
off

## The Vowel Sound in **saw**

Write the spelling word that completes each sentence.

5. You must _____ softly in a library.

6. Please turn _____ the stove.

7. These shoes are too _____ for me.

8. We _____ two beavers in the pond.

**33** orange
store
floor
four

## The Vowel Sound in **for**

Write the spelling word that belongs in each group.

9. two, three, _____

10. wall, ceiling, _____

Suzie's
SNACK SHOP

**11.** red, yellow, _____

**12.** shop, market, _____

---

**34** father
dark
party
are

## The Vowel Sound in jar

Write the spelling word for each clue.

**13.** This man has a child. _____

**14.** This word goes with **am** and **is**.

_____

**15.** If it is not light outside, it is this.

_____

**16.** You have this on your birthday.

_____

---

**35** longer
older
bigger
writer

## Words with er

Write the spelling word that completes each sentence and rhymes with the underlined word.

**17.** A snake is _____ and stronger than a worm.

**18.** A _____ needs light that is brighter than candle light.

**19.** Please hand me the _____ folder.

**20.** The _____ digger found the gold.

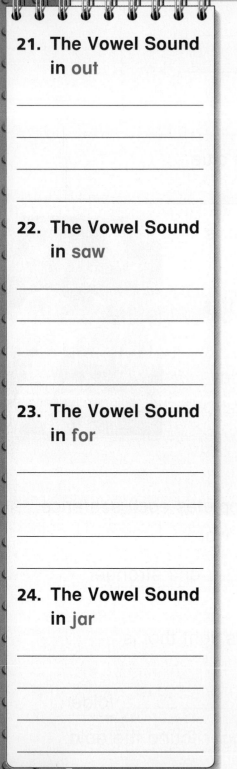

**21. The Vowel Sound in out**

_____

_____

_____

**22. The Vowel Sound in saw**

_____

_____

_____

_____

**23. The Vowel Sound in for**

_____

_____

_____

_____

**24. The Vowel Sound in jar**

_____

_____

_____

_____

# Review Sort

| orange | dark | town | floor |
| saw | out | party | store |
| are | father | four | flower |
| around | talk | off | small |

21. Write the **four** words that have the vowel sound in out. Circle the letters that spell the vowel sound in each word.

22. Write the **four** words that have the vowel sound in saw. Circle the letter or letters that spell the vowel sound in each word.

23. Write the **four** words that have the vowel sound in for. Circle the letter or letters that spell the vowel sound in each word.

24. Write the **four** words that have the vowel sound in jar. Circle the words that have ar.

These four er words have been sorted into two groups. Tell how the words in each group are alike.

25. **runner    bigger**

_____

_____

26. **writer    baker**

_____

_____

# Writer's Workshop

## A Description

A description of a person tells how that person looks, moves, and sounds. Study the beginning of Shawna's description of her new baby sister.

Yesterday Mom and Dad brought Katie home. At first I thought they left the baby at the hospital. The blanket looked empty. Then I saw a tiny pink hand pop out of the blanket. I got closer. I could hear little peeps. She looked like a bird.

**Prewriting** Shawna followed the steps in the writing process to describe her baby sister. She used a senses web to plan her writing. On it she listed details that told about her baby sister. Part of Shawna's web is shown here. Study what Shawna did.

The Baby

**See**
tiny pink hand
looked like a bird
no hair
wrinkled skin

## It's Your Turn!

Write your own description. You can describe a friend, a family member, or anyone you want. Plan your writing by making a senses web. Then follow the other steps in the writing process—writing, revising, proofreading, and publishing. Try to use spelling words from this lesson in your description.

# Commonly Misspelled Words

| | | | |
|---|---|---|---|
| about | family | name | their |
| above | favorite | nice | then |
| across | friend | now | there |
| again | friends | once | they |
| a lot | get | one | though |
| am | getting | our | time |
| and | girl | out | today |
| another | goes | outside | too |
| are | guess | party | two |
| because | have | people | upon |
| been | hear | play | very |
| before | her | please | want |
| beginning | here | pretty | was |
| bought | him | read | went |
| boy | his | really | were |
| buy | house | right | when |
| can | in | said | where |
| came | into | saw | white |
| children | know | scared | with |
| color | like | school | would |
| come | little | sent | write |
| didn't | made | some | writing |
| does | make | store | wrote |
| don't | me | swimming | your |
| every | my | teacher | you're |

# Spelling Table

## Consonants

| Sound | Example Words | Spellings |
|-------|--------------|-----------|
| b | big | b |
| ch | child, catch | ch tch |
| d | day, add | d dd |
| f | fast, off | f ff |
| g | get, egg | g gg |
| h | hand, who | h wh |
| j | jog, sponge | j g |
| k | can, keep, school, sick | c k ch ck |
| ks | six | x |
| kw | quit | qu |
| l | look, all | l ll |
| m | made, swimming, numb | m mm mb |
| n | not, running, knock | n nn kn |
| ng | thank, ring | n ng |
| p | pet, dropped | p pp |
| r | run, writer | wr |
| s | sat, dress, city | s ss c |
| sh | she | sh |
| t | ten, matter | t tt |
| th | that, thing | th |
| v | have, of | v f |
| w | went, whale, one | w wh o |
| y | you | y |
| z | zoo, blizzard, says | z zz s |

## Vowels

| Sound | Example Words | Spellings |
|-------|--------------|-----------|
| short a | cat, have | a a_e |
| long a | baby, take, play, nail, eight, they | a a_e ay ai eigh ey |
| ah | father, star | a |
| short e | red, tread, many, said, says | e ea a ai ay |
| long e | he, eat, tree, people, belief, very | e ea ee eo ie y |
| short i | is, give | i i_e |
| long i | find, ride, pie, high my, eye | i i_e ie igh y eye |
| short o | on, want | o a |
| long o | so, nose, road, boulder, snow | o o_e oa ou ow |
| oi | boy | oy |
| aw | off, call, haul, saw | o a au aw |
| o | corn, store, door, four | o o_e oo ou |
| long oo | zoo, blue, new, do, you | oo ue ew o ou |
| short oo | good, could, pull | oo ou u |
| ow | out, owl | ou ow |
| short u | run, brother | u o |

## Spelling Dictionary

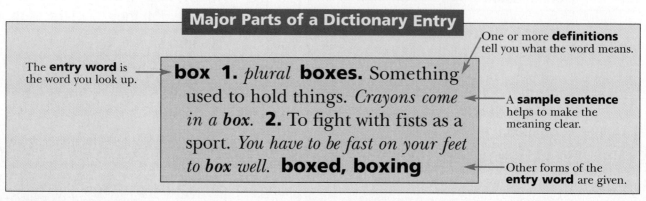

The **entry word** is the word you look up.

One or more **definitions** tell you what the word means.

**box 1.** *plural* **boxes.** Something used to hold things. *Crayons come in a box.* **2.** To fight with fists as a sport. *You have to be fast on your feet to box well.* **boxed, boxing**

A **sample sentence** helps to make the meaning clear.

Other forms of the **entry word** are given.

---

**active** Doing something most of the time; moving around; busy. *My active kitten never rests.*

**add** To put in as something extra. *I will add more milk to the batter for the cake.* **added, adding**

**adjust** To change so as to make right or better. *She will adjust the color on the television.* **adjusted, adjusting**

**admit** To say that something is true or a fact. *Did he admit that he made a mistake?* **admitted, admitting** *Thank you for admitting that you took the wrong jacket.*

**adopt 1.** To take and make one's own. *We will adopt the puppy and take it home.* **2.** To take a child born to another person into one's family and raise it as one's own. *My mother and father are going to adopt a baby. She will be my sister.* **adopted, adopting**

**advice** An idea someone else gives of how to fix a problem. *Please give me advice on how to win the game.*

**after** At a later time than. *I go to the park after school.*

**alert** To warn. *The bell will alert the class to come inside.* **alerted, alerting** *The red light was alerting us to stop.*

**all 1.** Every one of. *All the tadpoles turned into frogs.* **2.** Nothing but. *All I could think about was my birthday.*

**am** *I am glad to see you.* Look up **be.**

**amuse 1.** To entertain. *The puppet show will amuse the class.* **2.** To make laugh or smile. *My sister's jokes amuse me.* **amused, amusing** *He is amusing his father with funny stories.*

**an** Any, or one. *I ate an apple and a banana.*

**and** Added to; as well as. *What hides in a tree and eats peanuts? (A shy elephant)*

**any** One of several, but no special one. *You can take any bus to get to my house.*

**are** *Most elephants are gray.* Look up **be.**

**arm** *plural* **arms.** Part of the body between the hand and shoulder. *Your elbow is in the middle part of your arm.*

**around 1.** All over. *They traveled around the country.* **2.** In a circle. *We have a garden around our house.*

**art** *plural* **arts.** Paintings, drawings, or other beautiful things. *All my drawings are examples of great art.*

**ask** To question. *Ask me any riddle and I'll tell you the answer.* **asked, asking** *She asked her teacher a question.*

**ate** *I ate a peanut butter sandwich for lunch.* Look up **eat.**

**athlete** *plural* **athletes.** A person who plays sports. *The athlete is strong.*

**baby** *plural* **babies.** A young child or animal. *Brad had fuzz instead of hair when he was a baby.*

**baby sitter** *plural* **baby sitters.** A person who takes care of children when the parents are not at home. *The baby sitter plays games with the children.*

**back 1.** *plural* **backs.** Opposite of **front.** *Turn your back while I run and hide.* **2.** To a former place. *We go back to the lake every summer.*

**bacon** Salted and smoked meat that comes from the back and sides of a pig. *I had bacon for breakfast today.*

**bake** To cook in an oven. *Let's bake cookies this afternoon.* **baked, baking** *Mom baked bread for us. Dad is baking a special cake for my birthday party.*

**baker** *plural* **bakers.** Someone who cooks things in an oven. *A very good baker made this tasty bread!*

**ball** *plural* **balls.** Something round that is used in games. *Throw me the ball.*

**bamboo** *plural* **bamboos.** A tall grass. The long woody parts called stems are empty inside. They are often used to make fishing poles, chairs, and other things. *My chair made out of bamboo is light.*

**barber** *plural* **barbers.** A person who cuts hair and shaves beards. *The barber cuts my hair every six weeks.*

**barn** *plural* **barns.** A large shed. *Some farm animals live in a barn.*

**batch** *plural* **batches.** A group of things made at one time. *My sister made ten batches of cookies for my class at school.*

**be 1.** To equal in identity or meaning. *That girl is my sister.* **2.** To have or show a certain quality or characteristic. *I am tall and thin.* **3.** To belong to a certain group or class. *Whales are mammals.* **4.** To occupy a certain place or position. *Your book was here yesterday.* **5.** To live; to exist. *Once upon a time, there were three bears.* **6.** To take place; to happen. *Thanksgiving is next week.* **am, is, are; was, were, being, been. Be** verbs are also used as helping verbs. *I am teaching my dog a new trick.*

**bed** *plural* **beds.** A place to sleep. *How is a bed like an elephant? (It has a head and four legs.)*

**bee** *plural* **bees.** An insect with four wings, a hairy body, and usually a sting. *This kind of bee makes honey.*

**beggar** *plural* **beggars.** A person who asks other people for money, food, or clothes in order to live. *My mother gave the beggar some money.*

**beginner** *plural* **beginners.** A person who is starting to do or learn something for the first time. *Swimming lessons are important for a beginner in the water.*

**being** *Thank you for being so helpful.* Look up **be**.

**belief** *plural* **beliefs. 1.** Trust in someone or something. *I have belief in my father.* **2.** Something that one feels sure is true. *My belief is that we go to a fine school.*

**bell** *plural* **bells.** Something that rings when struck or pressed. *I think I heard the bell calling us for dinner.*

**best** *It was the best movie I'd ever seen.* Look up **good.**

**big** Large. *Yuko ate a big dinner after the game.* **bigger, biggest** *He ate a bigger dinner than we thought he would.*

**bike 1.** *plural* **bikes.** Something to ride on that has two wheels; a bicycle. *You move a bike by pedaling with your legs.* **2.** To ride a bike. *How far can you bike without getting tired?* **biked, biking**

**bitter** Having a sharp, biting, or bad taste. *The tea tasted bitter without sugar.* **bitterer, bitterest**

**black** *plural* **blacks.** The darkest of all colors. *Black is the color of coal.*

**blank 1.** *plural* **blanks.** An empty space. *Write your answer in the blank.* **2.** Without writing or marks. *I need some blank paper.* **3.** Empty. *There is a blank spot in the picture.* **blanker, blankest**

**blizzard** *plural* **blizzards.** A long, heavy storm of falling snow with very strong winds. *The roads were closed because of the blizzard.*

**block** *plural* **blocks. 1.** A city section or square. *My best friend lives on my block.* **2.** A solid object with flat sides. *A red block was missing from the toy box.*

**blue** *plural* **blues.** The color of the clear sky. *Blue is my favorite color.*

**blush** To become red in the face from feeling ashamed, nervous, or silly. *Sometimes I blush when I do not know the answer to a question.* **blushed, blushing**

**boat** *plural* **boats.** A small ship. *May we borrow your boat to go to the lake tomorrow?*

**bonnet** *plural* **bonnets.** A hat that is tied under the chin  with ribbons. *The baby looked cute in the white bonnet.*

**bony 1.** Made of or like bone. *The dinosaur skeleton is bony.* **2.** Full of bones. *The fish we had for dinner was very bony.* **3.** Very thin. *The bony dog was very hungry.* **bonier, boniest**

**book** *plural* **books.** Printed or blank pages fastened together between two covers. *This book has poems and fairy tales in it.*

**booth** *plural* **booths. 1.** A small stall where things are sold or shown. *Our club sold popcorn at our* **booth.** **2.** A small closed place. *We sat in a* **booth** *at the restaurant.*

**boulder** *plural* **boulders.** A very large, rounded rock. *We climbed on top of the* **boulder.**

**box 1.** *plural* **boxes.** Something used to hold things. *Crayons come in a* **box.** **2.** To fight with fists as a sport. *You have to be fast on your feet to* **box** *well.* **boxed, boxing**

**boy** *plural* **boys.** A male child. *That* **boy** *with red hair is my brother.*

**brave** Able to face danger without fear. *The* **brave** *mole protected her babies from the owl.* **braver, bravest** *The little animal was* **braver** *today than yesterday.*

**bravery** Ability to face danger or pain without fear; courage. *Firefighters show their* **bravery** *when they put out fires.*

**bring** To carry along with. *Be sure to* **bring** *your lunch to school tomorrow.* **brought, bringing**

**brother** *plural* **brothers.** A boy or man with the same parents as another person. *Sue and her* **brother** *take good care of their pets.*

**brow** *plural* **brows.** The forehead; the part of the face above the eyes. *His hair covered his* **brow.**

**buckle 1.** *plural* **buckles.** Something that fastens together one end of a belt or strap with the other end. *The* **buckle** *on the belt is gold.* **2.** To fasten with a buckle. *I always* **buckle** *my seat belt.* **buckled, buckling**

**buddy** *plural* **buddies.** A close friend. *My* **buddy** *and I like to go to the zoo.*

**bug** *plural* **bugs.** An insect. *Some* **bugs** *eat leaves.*

**bulletin** *plural* **bulletins.** A short notice of the latest news on radio, television, or in the newspaper. *The* **bulletin** *on television told us about the flooded streets.*

**bus** *plural* **buses** or **busses.** A large car with rows of seats. *The school* **bus** *stops on my corner.*

**bushel** *plural* **bushels.** A measure for dry things such as vegetables, fruit, and grain. *We picked a* **bushel** *of apples from our tree.*

**but 1.** Yet, still. *I planted the seeds,* **but** *they never grew.* **2.** Except. *The teacher gave everyone a note* **but** *me.*

**by 1.** Beyond, past. *Marie goes* **by** *my house every day.* **2.** Beside. *My house is right* **by** *the river.* **3.** Not later than. *Be home* **by** *six o'clock, please.*

**call 1.** To cry out. *Mom will call me when it's time to eat supper.* **2.** To telephone. *Call her up and see if you can eat here.* **called, calling**

**came** *Bob came to my house yesterday.* Look up **come.**

**can 1.** To know how to do something. *She can write her name in cursive.* **2.** To be able to. *I can run quickly.* **3.** To have permission. *My dad says we can go outside.* **could** *I knew I could swim across the pool.*

**cannon** *plural* **cannons** or **cannon.** A large, heavy gun that is put on wheels or some other base. *They fired a cannon in the park.*

**car** *plural* **cars.** An automobile. *My mom drove her car to the store.*

**cat** *plural* **cats.** A small furry animal. *Why is a cat a good pet? (Because it is purr-fect!)*

**catch 1.** A game played by throwing a ball. *Let's play catch over in the field.* **2.** To get hold of. *What can you catch but cannot throw? (A cold)* **caught, catching** *He is catching a butterfly with his net.*

**chain** *plural* **chains.** A number of rings joined together. *We used a chain to pull the truck out of the mud.*

**cheap** Low in cost. *The candy for one penny is cheap.* **cheaper, cheapest**

**cheat** To act in a way that is not honest or fair. *I will never cheat in school.* **cheated, cheating**

**child** *plural* **children.** A young boy or girl. *The teacher gave each child a book.*

**children** *There are twenty children in our second grade.* Look up **child.**

**chop** To cut up into small pieces. *He began to chop the wood into logs.* **chopped, chopping**

**city** *plural* **cities.** A large and important town. *There are many places to eat in a city.*

**claim 1.** To say that something is true. *They claim that they are the best team.* **2.** To ask for something that is one's own. *I will claim my coat at the door.* **claimed, claiming** *We claimed our package at the post office.*

**class** *plural* **classes.** A group of students. *Our class put on a play for the whole school.*

**classmate** *plural* **classmates.** A person in the same class at school. *My classmate and I have desks next to each other.*

**clean 1.** Not dirty. *It is hard to find a clean and shiny penny.* **cleaner, cleanest 2.** To take dirt from. *Neal will clean the window in his room.* **cleaned, cleaning**

**219**

**climate** *plural* **climates.** The way the weather of a place usually is. The climate includes how hot or cold it is and how much rain falls. *What is the climate in your city?*

**clock** *plural* **clocks.** Something that tells the time. *What has a face and two hands but does not speak? (A clock)*

**clover** *plural* **clovers.** A small plant with leaves that have three parts. Clover also has rounded bunches of small white, red, yellow, or purple flowers. *Cows eat clover.*

**clown** *plural* **clowns.** A person who does funny things to make people laugh. *A circus wouldn't be much fun without a clown.*

**club** *plural* **clubs. 1.** A group of people who like to do the same thing. *Our club is for people who want to learn about insects.* **2.** A stick. *In golf, you use a club to hit the ball.*

**coat** *plural* **coats.** Clothing with sleeves worn to keep warm. *I will wear a coat today. It is cold outside!*

**cocoon** *plural* **cocoons.** The silky case spun by a caterpillar or other young insect that keeps it safe  while it is becoming a moth, butterfly, or other adult insect. *The butterfly came out of its cocoon.*

**cold** Chilly, not hot. *It is so cold today that I had better wear my winter coat.* **colder, coldest** *It is colder than yesterday.*

**come** To move towards; to arrive. *She will come over.* **came, coming** *Tanya came to my house for dinner.*

**cook 1.** *plural* **cooks.** A person who prepares food. *Norma is a good cook. She always has great things to eat!* **2.** To prepare food. *I don't like to cook. I would rather eat at Tien's house.* **cooked, cooking**

**cookbook** *plural* **cookbooks.** A book that tells how to make and cook food. *The cookbook told how to make a cherry pie.*

**cookie** *plural* **cookies.** Small, sweet cakes. *Maria makes good chocolate chip cookies.*

**corn 1.** A plant with large ears of grain. *The corn grows tall in the summer.* **2.** A yellow grain. *Corn is my favorite vegetable.*

**could** *My pet frog could jump ten feet!* Look up **can.**

**cow** *plural* **cows.** A female farm animal that gives milk. *The farmer milks the cow every day.*

**coward** *plural* **cowards.** A person who is not brave or is afraid to do hard or dangerous things. *Kiesha proved she was not a coward when she got the cat out of the tree.*

**craft** *plural* **crafts.** Skill in making something with the hands. *Making baskets is a craft.*

**cry 1.** To shed tears. *He fell on his head and began to cry.* **2.** To shout. *His friend had to cry out for help.* **cried, crying**

**cut 1.** *plural* **cuts.** An opening made with a sharp edge. *Do you have a bandage for the cut on Rosa's toe?* **2.** To make an opening in. *She cut herself on Nat's roller skate.* **3.** To divide. *We need scissors to cut the string into pieces.* **cut, cutting** *We are cutting the melon into several slices.*

**dainty** Pretty in a small, thin, soft, or light way. *The ring is very dainty.* **daintier, daintiest**

**dark** Having no light. *Stars show up well on a dark night.* **darker, darkest**

**delay 1.** *plural* **delays.** Time while something is being put off. *There was a delay in the game.* **2.** To put off. *The teacher will delay the test.* **delayed, delaying**

**deny** To say that something is not true. *The children deny breaking the big window.* **denied, denying** *Hector keeps denying that he is the best player.*

**depart** To leave; go away. *The visitors plan to depart tomorrow morning.* **departed, departing**

**desk** *plural* **desks.** A table on which to write. *Olivia has a hundred crayons in her desk!*

**diet** *plural* **diets.** The things a person or animal eats and drinks most of the time. *Worms are part of that bird's diet.*

**dipper** *plural* **dippers.** A cup with a long handle that is used to lift water, soup, or other liquids. *The dipper for the soup is next to the pot.*

**disease** *plural* **diseases.** Sickness; illness. *A cold is a disease.*

**dislike 1.** *plural* **dislikes.** A feeling of not liking something. *I have a dislike for rainy days.* **2.** To have a feeling of not liking something. *Do you dislike the play?* **disliked, disliking** *We disliked the games they played at the party.*

**do** To work at a job. *Do all the math problems on page 5, please.* **did, doing**

**dodge** To miss something by moving away quickly. *Birds dodge the trees when they fly.* **dodged, dodging**

**dog** *plural* **dogs.** A four-footed animal. *My dog likes to bark at my cat.*

**door** *plural* **doors.** A piece of wood, metal, or glass that moves to let people in and out. *What goes through a **door** but never comes inside? (A key)*

**dot 1.** *plural* **dots.** A very small round point. *Her best dress is white with red **dots** on it.* **2.** To mark with a round point. *Be sure to **dot** an i when you write it.* **dotted, dotting** *She **dotted** the paper with green ink.*

**draw** To make a picture. *Jill will **draw** a picture of you if you ask her.* **drew, drawing**

**dream 1.** *plural* **dreams.** Something seen during sleep. *Don't you hate the alarm to wake you up in the middle of a good **dream?*** **2.** To think or see something during sleep. *Children sometimes **dream** about school.* **dreamed, dreaming**

**dress 1.** *plural* **dresses.** Clothing worn by a girl or woman. *Lan's favorite **dress** has a yellow skirt.* **2.** To put clothes on. *Ricardo's little brother is unable to **dress** himself yet.* **dressed, dressing** *My sister is **dressing** her doll in a new outfit.*

**drop 1.** *plural* **drops.** A round-shaped bit of water or other liquid. *The rain fell in heavy **drops** against the window.* **2.** To let fall. *Kevin was afraid he would **drop** the heavy pail.* **dropped, dropping** *Erin **dropped** the dish, and it broke. I keep **dropping** my keys.*

**drought** *plural* **droughts.** A long time with little or no rain. *The plants began to dry up because of the **drought**.*

**duckling** *plural* **ducklings.** A baby duck. *The **ducklings** walked in a line behind their mother.*

**eat** To swallow food. *A toad will **eat** one hundred insects a day if it can catch them!* **ate, eating**

**egg** *plural* **eggs.** A special cell formed in the body of a female animal. *All those baby chicks hatched from **eggs**.*

**eight** *plural* **eights.** The number after seven, written 8. *Many second-grade children are **eight** years old.*

**end 1.** *plural* **ends.** The finish of something. *We go back to school at the **end** of summer.* **2.** To stop. *In June, it seems as if the summer will never **end**.* **ended, ending** *We left the soccer field when the game **ended**.*

**explode** To burst or cause to burst suddenly with a loud noise; blow up. *A balloon will **explode** if you put too much air into it.* **exploded, exploding**

**eye** *plural* **eyes.** The part of the body used to see. *The hammerhead shark has one **eye** at each end of its head.*

**fade** **1.** To lose or make to lose color. *The dress may **fade** after it is washed.* **2.** To become less fresh. *Flowers **fade** if they are not put in water.* **faded, fading**

**faithful** Able to be trusted and counted on; always there. *His **faithful** dog always meets him at the school bus.*

**false** **1.** Not true or correct; wrong. *His answer was **false**.* **2.** Not real. *Some people have **false** teeth.* **falser, falsest**

**far** At a distance. *I live **far** from school. I have to walk a long way.*

**farm** *plural* **farms.** Land and buildings in the country. *Crops are grown on a **farm**.*

**farmer** *plural* **farmers.** A person who grows crops or raises animals. *Why did the **farmer** name his pig Ink? (Because the pig kept running out of the pen)*

**fast** Not slow; speedy. *She ran by fast.* **faster, fastest** *She is a faster runner than I.*

**father** *plural* **fathers.** A male parent. *Jessie's **father** has a beard.*

**faucet** *plural* **faucets.** A part made for turning water on and off from a pipe or sink; tap. *Please turn off the **faucet** after watering the plants.*

**feet** *My **feet** hurt from standing all day.* Look up **foot**.

**fill** To make full. *Please **fill** the glass with milk.* **filled, filling**

**find** To come upon by chance. *I cannot **find** my glasses.* **found, finding**

**fish** **1.** *plural* **fish** or **fishes.** A water animal that has fins and breathes through gills. *The whale shark is the biggest **fish** in the sea.* **2.** To catch fish. *This seems to be a good spot to **fish**.* **fished, fishing** *We **fished** for trout when we were at the lake last week.*

**five** *plural* **fives.** The number after four, written 5. *Three plus two is **five**.*

**flat** Level. *A **flat** pan is good for making pancakes.* **flatter, flattest** *A pan is **flatter** than a bowl.*

**floor** *plural* **floors.** The part of a room that is walked on.
*Ned: What was the hardest thing about roller-skating?*
*Ted: The **floor**!*

**flower** *plural* **flowers.** A blossom. *A tulip is a kind of **flower**.*

**fly 1.** *plural* **flies.** An insect with one pair of wings. *A fly makes a nice lunch for a spider.* **2.** To move through the air. *Most birds fly south when winter comes.* **flew, flying**

**food** *plural* **foods.** Something to eat. *Bring plenty of food to eat at the picnic!*

**foot** *plural* **feet.** Part of the leg. *People have five toes on each foot.*

**for 1.** Fitting the need. *This bike is good for riding long distances.* **2.** Helping someone. *I'll get the bike for you.*

**found** *I found a dime on the way to school.* Look up **find.**

**four** *plural* **fours.** The number after three, written 4. *Two plus two is four.*

**freeze** To harden from a liquid to a solid because of the cold. *Water will freeze into ice.* **froze, freezing**

**frog** *plural* **frogs.** A small green animal with webbed feet. *A frog lives near water.*

**from 1.** Starting at. *I just flew in from South America.* **2.** Out of. *Did you get that pencil from the desk?*

**full** Holding all that it can hold. *When rivers get full, they sometimes flood.* **fuller, fullest**

**fun** A good time. *Everyone had lots of fun at Rita's circus party.*

**funny 1.** Causing laughter. *Alice told a funny joke in school today.* **2.** Strange. *Miss Lea gave Anita a funny look.* **funnier, funniest**

**gain** To increase. *How much weight did your puppy gain?* **gained, gaining**

**game** *plural* **games.** A contest played with rules. *Chess is a game for two people to play.*

**gave** *I gave my brother colored pencils for his birthday.* Look up **give.**

**get** To come to have by earning, buying or receiving. *I get a dollar for my allowance.* **got, getting** *I got a present for my birthday.*

**girl** *plural* **girls.** A female child. *That girl is my sister.*

**give** To hand over. *What do you give an elephant that has a lot of clothes? (Another trunk)* **gave, giving** *I am giving you this pen and pencil.*

**glimpse 1.** *plural* **glimpses.** A quick look. *Did you get a glimpse of the pretty bird?* **2.** To get a quick look. *I was able to glimpse the clown in the car.* **glimpsed, glimpsing**

**go** To move from one place to another. *Morris had to go home early. He has chicken pox.* **went, going**

**goat** *plural* **goats.** An animal with short horns and a beard. *Why is it hard to talk when there is a goat around? (Because it keeps butting in)*

**gold** A yellow metal. *Gold is used for making coins and jewelry.*

**good** Fine, excellent. *It is a good idea to get to school on time.* **better, best**

**got** *Billy got a pogo stick for his birthday.* Look up **get.**

**green** *plural* **greens.** The color of growing plants. *My shirt has green in it.*

**grow** **1.** To get bigger. *Puppies grow into dogs.* **2.** To plant and care for. *We grow tomatoes and lettuce in our garden.* **grew, growing**

**guilt** **1.** A feeling of shame for having done something wrong. *I felt guilt after I hit my friend with a ball.* **2.** The fact of having done something wrong. *He admitted his guilt for telling a lie.*

**habit** *plural* **habits.** Something that a person does so often that it is done without thinking. *I have a habit of brushing my teeth before I go to bed.*

**had** *Juan's gerbil had a fancy cage.* Look up **have.**

**hand** **1.** *plural* **hands.** The part of the arm below the wrist. *There are four fingers and a thumb on your hand.* **2.** To do something with the hand. *Please hand me a peach.* **handed, handing** *Holly handed her dad the tool.*

**happy** Glad. *Ernesto is happy that he found his glove.* **happier, happiest**

**harmful** Causing hurt; bad for. *Smoking can be harmful to a person's health.*

**has** *What has four legs and a trunk? (A mouse on vacation)* Look up **have.**

**haul** **1.** To carry or move from one place to another. *The truck will haul away the logs.*  **2.** To pull or drag something heavy. *We had to haul the mattress up the stairs.* **hauled, hauling**

**have** **1.** To own. *Harry and Lou have four gerbils.* **2.** To go through. *The gerbils have fun running in the tunnels.* **had, having, has**

**he** A boy, man, or male animal. *He became the king.*

**heat** **1.** Warmth. *The heat from the sun feels good after swimming.* **2.** To warm. *Glen will heat the soup on the stove.* **heated, heating**

**225**

**help** To do something useful. *Would you **help** me move these boxes, please?* **helped, helping** *They were **helping** me clean my room.*

**helper** *plural* **helpers.** Someone who does something useful. *Ling will help me teach swimming. She will be my **helper**.*

**her** **1.** Belonging to a female. *Janet gave **her** brother a red T-shirt.* **2.** A girl, woman, or female animal. *I saw **her** in the store.*

**hid** *They ran and **hid**. We couldn't find them anywhere!* Look up **hide.**

**hide** To put or to go out of sight. *Why do elephants **hide** behind trees? (To scare ants)* **hid, hiding**

**high** Far above the ground. *The balloon floated **high** up in the sky.* **higher, highest**

**hill** *plural* **hills.** A raised part of the earth. A mound. *Why do giraffes roll down the **hill**? (They can't roll up it very well!)*

**him** A boy, man, or male animal. *Jetta gave **him** a T-shirt. She told **him** to wear it to school.*

**his** Belonging to a male. *Ella's brother wears **his** red shirt all the time.*

**hold** **1.** To keep back. *We used a heavy stone to **hold** the door open.* **2.** To keep in the hand. *Will you **hold** my books while I open the door?* **held, holding**

**hole** *plural* **holes.** An opening. *A woodchuck lives in a **hole** in the ground.*

**home** *plural* **homes.** The place where a person or animal lives. *A bee's **home** is in a hive.*

**hop** To move up and down quickly. *We like to **hop** over the cracks in the sidewalk.* **hopped, hopping** *The rabbit **hopped** through the grass. The frog is **hopping** across the grass.*

**hope** To wish. *I **hope** I remember all my spelling words today!* **hoped, hoping** *Mei **hoped** for a sunny day.*

**hopeful** Having, feeling, or showing hope. *We are **hopeful** that our team will win today.*

**horse** *plural* **horses.** A large, strong animal with hooves. *My **horse** has strong legs and can run very fast.*

**hot** Very warm. *There are many **hot** days in summer.* **hotter, hottest**

**house** *plural* **houses.** A place where people or animals live. *Five people live at my **house**.*

**how** **1.** In what way? ***How** do you keep cool at a ball game? (Sit near a fan!)* **2.** For what amount? ***How** much do these tickets cost?*

**ice** Frozen water. *In winter, it is fun to skate on the ice on the pond.*

**inside** Into. *Go inside the house if it rains.*

**insult** **1.** *plural* **insults.** Rude words or actions that can hurt someone's feelings. *It was an insult when you did not wave to me.* **2.** To hurt the feelings of someone by speaking or acting rudely toward that person. *He said he would try not to insult anyone.* **insulted, insulting**

**jar** *plural* **jars.** A glass with a lid. *Ellie gave us a jar of jam she had made.*

**jet** *plural* **jets.** **1.** A stream that squirts from a small hole. *He got me wet with a jet from his water pistol!* **2.** An aircraft. *I put him on a jet to visit his grandmother.*

**job** *plural* **jobs.** Work. *I would like to have a job working in an ice cream store.*

**jog** To run at a slow, steady trot. *He likes to jog to school.* **jogged, jogging** *We jogged around the track.*

**joke** **1.** *plural* **jokes.** A funny story. *Alice made us laugh with her joke.* **2.** To tell funny stories. *Sometimes Alice jokes too much.* **joked, joking** *He was joking when he said he broke my toy.*

**jump** To leap. *That animal can jump as high as 30 feet.* **jumped, jumping**

**jumper** *plural* **jumpers.** Someone or something that leaps. *You have to be a good jumper to get across that wide brook.*

**just** Exactly. *This shirt is just the right size for me.*

**keep** **1.** To own. *You may keep this toy.* **2.** To stay. *Please keep off the grass.* **3.** To store. *I keep my toys in a chest.* **4.** To continue in the same way. *Keep walking until you see the blue house.* **kept, keeping**

**kept** *The children kept playing, even though it was time to go home.* Look up **keep.**

**know** To be sure. *How do you know when there's an elephant in your bathtub? (You can smell the wet peanuts.)* **knew, knowing**

**land 1.** *plural* **lands.** The part of the earth not covered by water. *You cannot see* **land** *from the middle of the big lake.* **2.** To arrive by ship or plane. *They will* **land** *at the airport at four o'clock.* **landed, landing**

**last 1.** Final. *The* **last** *letter in the alphabet is z.* **2.** Just before now. *I have been practicing for the* **last** *two hours!* **3.** To continue a long time. *I hope my legs* **last** *until the race is over.* **lasted, lasting**

**leap 1.** *plural* **leaps.** A jump. *That frog took a huge* **leap** *and jumped out of the pond!* **2.** To jump. *The salmon is a fish that can* **leap** *up waterfalls!* **leaped, leaping**

**liberty** *plural* **liberties.** Freedom. *The whale was given its* **liberty.**

**license** *plural* **licenses.** A paper or card showing that the law says a person may do something. *My sister just got her driver's* **license.**

**lie 1.** To be in a flat position. *I need to* **lie** *down and take a nap.* **lay, lying 2.** Something that is not true. *Don't tell your mother a* **lie.**

**like 1.** Almost the same. *People say I look* **like** *a movie star.* **2.** To enjoy. *I would* **like** *to act in movies.* **liked, liking** *I* **liked** *the chocolate ice cream the best.*

**lining** *plural* **linings.** A coating or covering for the inside of something. *The coat had a fur* **lining** *to make it warmer.*

**lion** *plural* **lions.** A large, powerful animal related to the cat. *The* **lion** *stood up and gave a loud roar.*

**live 1.** To be alive. *Fish cannot* **live** *out of water.* **2.** To stay, as at home. *What would it be like to* **live** *in a tree house?* **lived, living** *We* **lived** *in the city for many years. They are* **living** *next door to us.*

**lobster** *plural* **lobsters.** A sea animal that has a hard shell and five pairs of legs. The front pair are large claws. *I like to eat* **lobster.**

**long** Great in distance, time, or length. *We drove a* **long** *way to go to the beach.* **longer, longest** *The dog's legs are* **longer** *than the cat's legs.*

**look** To see. *Look at that strange bird!* **looked, looking**

**lost** Missing. *Ann's pet turtle is* **lost.** *Have you seen it?*

**love 1.** *plural* **loves.** A strong liking. *Give them my* **love.** **2.** To feel a strong liking. *Leon's uncle* **loves** *to cook.* **loved, loving**

**lunch** *plural* **lunches.** The meal eaten at midday. *We eat **lunch** in the cafeteria.*

**mail** Letters and packages sent through the post office. ***Mail** is not delivered on Sundays.*

**man** *plural* **men.** A grown male person. *The **man** with Jessie is her father.*

**many** A large number. *Clifton has **many** friends.* **more, most**

**mark** *plural* **marks. 1.** A spot on something. *A wet glass will leave a **mark** on a table.* **2.** A grade given in school. *I got good **marks** on my report card.*

**matter 1.** To be of importance. *It doesn't **matter** if we go sledding before or after lunch.* **2.** *plural* **matters.** Trouble or problem. *What's the **matter** with your foot?*

**maybe** Perhaps, possibly. ***Maybe** Miss Lee will forget to give us the math test tomorrow.*

**mean 1.** Unkind. *They were **mean** to laugh at Andy's mistakes.* **meaner, meanest 2.** To express the idea of. *A dictionary tells what words **mean**.* **meant, meaning**

**melon** *plural* **melons.** A large sweet fruit that grows on a vine and has a hard skin. *I had **melon** for breakfast.*

**memory** *plural* **memories.**
**1.** The power to remember things. *An elephant has a good **memory**.*
**2.** Something that is remembered. *One **memory** I have from this year is the field trip to the zoo.*

**men** *The **men** sang loudly in their deep voices.* Look up **man.**

**method** *plural* **methods.** A way of doing something. *I learned a new **method** of painting pictures.*

**mine** Belonging to me. *This sled is **mine**. I got it for my birthday.*

**mold 1.** *plural* **molds.** A form with space inside that is used to make something into a special shape. *Water will take the shape of a **mold** when it freezes.* **2.** To make into a special shape. *In art we tried to **mold** clay.* **molded, molding**

**monster** *plural* **monsters.**
**1.** A scary creature that is not real. *A picture of the **monster** was in the book.* **2.** A very large animal, plant, or thing. *The huge shark may seem like a **monster** to other fish.*

**moon** *plural* **moons.** A body that moves around a planet. *Our moon moves around the earth 365 times in a year.*

**more** **1.** Greater in amount. *There is more water in the world than there is land.* **2.** An additional amount. *May I have some more milk, please?*

**most** Greatest number or amount. *The team that scores the most points will win.*

**mother** *plural* **mothers.** A female parent. *My mother asked me to fasten my seat belt.*

**mouse** *plural* **mice.** A small gray animal with soft fur. *A mouse is about seven inches long.*

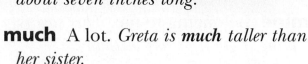

**much** A lot. *Greta is much taller than her sister.*

**mud** Soft and sticky earth. *Mud on your shoes makes a mess in the house!*

**my** Belonging to me. *My birthday is in December.*

**nail** *plural* **nails.** **1.** The growth at the end of a finger or toe. *I broke a nail when I fell down.* **2.** A thin, pointed metal pin. *You can fasten pieces of wood together with a nail.*

**name** **1.** *plural* **names.** A word by which a person or thing is called. *A good name for a poodle is Curly.* **2.** To give a name to. *What shall we name our cat?* **named, naming** *We named our bird Tweety.*

**napkin** *plural* **napkins.** A piece of cloth or paper used at meals to keep clothes clean and to wipe the mouth and hands. *I put my napkin in my lap to catch spills.*

**new** **1.** Recently made, grown, or invented. *Every year birds grow new feathers.* **2.** Never used. *We are going to put up new birdhouses this spring.* **newer, newest**

**next** **1.** Nearest or closest to. *Her puppy slept next to her.* **2.** Coming right after. *Turn to the next page.*

**nine** *plural* **nines.** The number after eight, written 9. *The number after nine is ten.*

**no** Not so. Opposite of **yes**. *No, I do not like spinach.*

**nose** *plural* **noses.** The part of the body used for breathing. *The elephant uses its trunk as a nose.*

**not** In no way. *Morris is not going with us.*

**now** At the present time. *May we go out and play now? It has stopped raining.*

**numb** Not able to feel or move. *My face is numb from the cold.* **number, numbest**

**of** **1.** Made from. *Many birds live in nests **of** twigs.* **2.** Holding. *May I borrow your box **of** crayons?*

**off** **1.** Away from. *He rode **off**.* **2.** Not on or connected. *She took **off** her coat.*

**old** Alive for a long time; not young. *The big elm tree is very **old**.* **older, oldest** *It is **older** than the pine tree.*

**on** **1.** Upon, touching. *Please put your coat **on** a hanger, not **on** the floor!* **2.** Growing upon. *Kevin's brand-new sneakers gave him blisters **on** his feet.*

**one** **1.** *plural* **ones.** The first and the least number, written 1. ***One** comes before two.* **2.** Single person or thing. *When two teams play a game, only **one** can win.*

**open** To make no longer shut or closed. *Why is a piano so hard to **open**? (All the keys are inside.)* **opened, opening**

**or** Word that shows you may choose. *Shall we go to the movies **or** stay home?*

**orange** *plural* **oranges.** **1.** A round, dark-yellow fruit. *An **orange** is good to eat. **Oranges** give juice, too.* **2.** The color of this fruit. *My bike is painted **orange**. Cars can see me on the road.*

**orchard** *plural* **orchards.** A place where fruit trees are grown. *My class picked many apples at the apple **orchard**.*

**organ** *plural* **organs.** A large musical instrument made of long and short pipes. The pipes make sounds when air is blown through them. A person pushes keys and pedals to make the air blow. *It takes hands and feet to play an **organ**.*

**other** Different. *She went into the **other** room.*

**our** Belonging to us. *This is **our** garden. We take care of it all summer.*

**out** Not inside. *The cat was **out** all night.*

**over** **1.** Across. *Let's see if we can jump **over** the river.* **2.** On top of. *No. Let's put a board **over** the water instead.* **3.** Above. *I think the water might be **over** our heads!*

**owl** *plural* **owls.** A bird with a flat face and hooked beak. *Owls sleep during the day and hunt at night.*

**ox** *plural* **oxen.** A male animal of the cattle family. *A strong **ox** is a useful farm animal.*

**pail** *plural* **pails.** A bucket. *The pail of water was so heavy that we dropped it and spilled all the water.*

**paint 1.** *plural* **paints.** Something to color with. *We bought blue paint for the walls in my room.* **2.** To cover something with paint. *Please don't paint our front porch and steps purple!* **painted, painting**

**painter** *plural* **painters.** Someone who puts colors on cloth, paper, or buildings. *The painters are working on our house. They are painting it white.*

**party** *plural* **parties.** People getting together for fun. *May I invite eight people to my party?*

**peach** *plural* **peaches.** A sweet, juicy fruit. *A peach tastes very good.*

**pedal 1.** *plural* **pedals.** A part that is moved by the foot to work something. *I put a new pedal on my bike.* **2.** To use or work a pedal. *It is hard to pedal up the hill.* **pedaled, pedaling**

**penny** *plural* **pennies.** One cent. *A penny is made of copper.*

**people** Human beings. *Many people watched the parade march down the street.*

**pick 1.** To choose. *Did you pick the brown puppy or the black-and-white one?* **2.** To gather. *He went out to the garden to pick flowers.* **picked, picking** *We are picking berries off the vines.*

**pie** *plural* **pies.** Fruit, custard, or meat in a crust. *For dessert we had peach pie.*

**play 1.** *plural* **plays.** A story acted on a stage. *I hope I get a good part in the play.* **2.** To take part in a game. *It takes 22 people to play football.* **3.** To have fun. *Will you play at my house?* **played, playing**

**please** Be so kind as to. *Please come to the store with me.*

**pond** *plural* **ponds.** A small body of water. *A pond is a good place to go swimming.*

**profit** *plural* **profits.** The money that a business makes after all its costs are paid. *We spent five dollars on lemons, cups, and sugar. We made ten dollars selling lemonade. Our profit was five dollars.*

**prop** To keep from falling by putting something under or against. *I propped the stuffed bear up with a pillow.* **propped, propping**

**pull** To tug. *A strong engine can pull a long train.* **pulled, pulling**

**pupil**[1] *plural* **pupils.** A person who has a teacher. *The pupil learned how to add.*

**pupil**[2] *plural* **pupils.** The black opening in the center of the eye where light enters. *The pupil of his eye was wide open.*

**puppy** *plural* **puppies.** A young dog. *I took my new puppy for a walk.*

**put** To set something in a place. *Please put the crayons away when you are through drawing.* **put, putting**

**rain 1.** *plural* **rains.** Water that falls from clouds. *I got wet when I played in the rain.* **2.** To fall in drops from clouds. *I wish it would never rain on weekends.* **rained, raining**

**recess** *plural* **recesses.** A short time for rest or play. *Recess at our school is a lot of fun.*

**rest 1.** What is left. *If you will wash half the dishes, I will do the rest.* **2.** To be still. *After we do the dishes, we can rest.* **rested, resting**

**rhyme 1.** *plural* **rhymes.** Sameness in the final sounds of words. **2.** To sound alike. *Old rhymes with cold.* **rhymed, rhyming**

**ride** To be carried. *It is exciting to ride on a roller coaster.* **rode, riding** *She is riding her horse on the beach.*

**ring 1.** *plural* **rings.** Something to wear on a finger. *Clara lost her gold ring.* **2.** To make a loud, clear sound. *Did the alarm ring?* **rang, ringing**

**road** *plural* **roads.** A street. *Is this the road to town?*

**rock 1.** *plural* **rocks.** Solid stone. *Much of the earth is rock.* **2.** To move gently back and forth. *A baby goes to sleep when you rock it.* **rocked, rocking**

**roll 1.** *plural* **rolls.** A bun. *These rolls are good. Hui baked them.* **2.** To move by turning over and over. *Catch the ball! It's going to roll down the hill!* **rolled, rolling**

**room** *plural* **rooms.** A space in a building. *The best place in our house is my room!*

**rope** *plural* **ropes.** Heavy string. *We used a rope to tie up our boat during the storm.*

**round** Shaped like a ball. *The earth is round.* **rounder, roundest**

**run** To move quickly. *Horses can run fast.* **ran, running** *Erin is running around the track.*

**runner** *plural* **runners.** Someone who moves quickly. *The best runner will win the race.*

**said** *I said I would like to come to his party.* Look up **say.**

**sail 1.** *plural* **sails.** A piece of cloth spread to catch the wind. *A big sail can make a boat move quickly.* **2.** To move smoothly. *Boats look pretty as they sail on the river.* **sailed, sailing**

**sang** *The birds sang at five o'clock in the morning and woke me.* Look up **sing.**

**saw** *Ming saw her friends coming out of school.* Look up **see.**

**say** To speak. *What do you say when you meet a two-headed monster? ("Hello, hello.")* **said, saying, says**

**says** *He says the party started an hour ago!* Look up **say.**

**school** *plural* **schools.** A place of teaching and learning. *We go to school to learn about all kinds of things.*

**see** To look at. *Matt can see the school from his house.* **saw, seeing**

**sell** To trade for money. *We will sell lemonade.* **sold, selling** *Mrs. Kang sold her bike for thirty dollars.*

**send 1.** To mail. *Don't forget to send us a postcard.* **2.** To cause to go. *I'll send Chris to the post office to get the mail.* **sent, sending**

**seven** *plural* **sevens.** The number after six, written 7. *Seven is an odd number.*

**she** A girl, woman, or female animal. *Nell says that she will go with us.*

**shelf** *plural* **shelves.** A flat, narrow piece of wood or metal to put things on. *Mimi keeps her books on a shelf over her desk.*

**ship** *plural* **ships.** **1.** A large boat. *My family came to America by ship.* **2.** An airplane or spacecraft. *The large ship flew across the sky.*

**shop 1.** *plural* **shops.** A place to buy things. *Wen's favorite place on Main Street is the ice cream shop.* **2.** To look for things in stores. *She likes to shop for birthday presents.* **shopped, shopping** *Alex shopped for the perfect shirt. We went shopping for groceries.*

**shopper** *plural* **shoppers.** Someone who visits stores. *It is wise to be a careful shopper.*

**short 1.** Not far. *I live near school. It is only a short walk.* **2.** Not tall. *I am too short to reach the top shelf.* **shorter, shortest**

**should** To have a duty to. *People should take good care of their pets.*

**side** *plural* **sides. 1.** A part of something. *Ming can kick a football to the other side of the field.* **2.** One of two or more groups. *I hope I will be playing on Ed's side in the game.*

**sing** To make music by using the voice. *Let's sing the ABC song.* **sang, singing** *She sang the baby to sleep.*

**sister** *plural* **sisters.** A girl or woman with the same parents as another. *Marty has a baby sister.*

**six** *plural* **sixes.** The number after five, written 6. *Three plus three is six.*

**skunk** *plural* **skunks.** A small black-and-white striped animal with a bushy tail. *A skunk protects itself with a strong, bad-smelling spray.*

**sky** *plural* **skies.** The upper air above the earth. *Do those clouds in the sky mean rain?*

**small** Little. *Children start out small. Then they grow big!* **smaller, smallest**

**snail** *plural* **snails.** A slow animal with a soft body and a shell. *We saw a snail on the sand at the beach.*

**snore** *plural* **snores.** A loud noise made while asleep. *If you hear a snore, you know that someone is sound asleep.*

**snow** *plural* **snows.** Soft white flakes of frozen water. *Snow covered the ground like a white blanket.*

**so 1.** To such a point. *Alice's joke was so funny we could not stop laughing.* **2.** Therefore. *Martin was sick, so he missed school today.*

**sold** *Beto sold his car. He needed money for college.* Look up **sell.**

**song** *plural* **songs.** A piece of music. *"Jingle Bells" is an easy song to sing.*

**soon** A short time from now. *The clouds are going away. It will stop raining soon.*

**sound** *plural* **sounds.** A noise. *An owl can fly without making a sound.*

**sponge** *plural* **sponges. 1.** A cleaning pad that soaks up water easily. *I used a sponge to clean the tub.* **2.** A water animal with a soft body that has holes and soaks up water. *I have never seen a live sponge.*

**spot 1.** *plural* **spots.** A small mark. *What could have made that ugly spot on the rug?* **2.** A place. *We always keep our ink in the same spot on top of the desk.* **3.** To make a mark on something. *Nothing will spot worse than ink!* **spotted, spotting** *The punch spotted the carpet when it spilled.*

**spring** *plural* **springs.** The season between winter and summer. *Flowers bloom in spring.*

**stand** To be upright on the feet. *We stand in line to buy our movie tickets.* **stood, standing** *The baby surprised us and stood all by herself.*

**star** *plural* **stars. 1.** The sun and other bright heavenly bodies. *The star we see best at night is the North Star.* **2.** A leading actor or actress, athlete, or musician. *My brother is a super drummer. I think he will be a rock star!*

**stay** To remain in one place, wait. *Please stay in your seats until the bell rings.* **stayed, staying**

**stone** *plural* **stones.** A small rock. *Don't trip on that stone in the path!*

**stood** *The horses stood in the shade.* Look up **stand.**

**stop** To finish, end. *You may stop studying at 7:00.* **stopped, stopping** *We stopped playing outside when it got dark. Mr. Johnson said he saw the truck stopping at the red light.*

**store** *plural* **stores.** A place where things are sold. *There is a large toy store in the city.*

**storm** *plural* **storms.** Very bad weather. *It is best to stay inside during a storm.*

**story** *plural* **stories.** A tale. *My mom reads me a story every night at bedtime.*

**street** *plural* **streets.** A road in a city or town. *The street in front of a house is noisy sometimes.*

**strut** To walk like a very important person. *Did you see Jake strut across the stage?* **strutted, strutting** *The winning team was strutting across the field.*

**such** Very. *Those are such pretty flowers.*

**summer** *plural* **summers.** The season of the year between spring and autumn. *We had fun at the beach last summer.*

**sun** *plural* **suns.** The closest star to Earth. *Earth and eight other planets move around the sun.*

**swim** To move through the water by using arms and legs. *You should know how to swim before going out in a boat.* **swam, swimming**

**tail** *plural* **tails.** The rear part of something. *I did not mean to step on the cat's tail.*

**take 1.** To grasp and hold. *The clerk will take my money.* **2.** To travel on or go by way of. *We take the train to our grandma's house.* **took, taking** *Our class took a bus to the zoo.*

**talk** To speak words. *What is the best way to **talk** to a monster? (Long distance)* **talked, talking**

**tell** To say in words. *Karen will **tell** her mom a joke.* **told, telling** *My mom **told** me to hurry and clean my room.*

**ten** *plural* **tens.** The number after nine, written 10. *Five plus five is **ten.***

**than** Compared with. *Is a pound of books heavier **than** a pound of feathers? (No. They weigh the same!)*

**thank** To say that one is grateful. *Don't forget to **thank** Uncle Elroy for the nice shirt.* **thanked, thanking** *I **thanked** everyone for coming to my party.*

**that** **1.** Something or someone at a distance. ***That** man over there is my uncle, not this one.* **2.** Used to connect words in a sentence. *I am afraid **that** he is lost.*

**the** A definite thing. *Who broke **the** window? There's a football in **the** living room!*

**them** People, animals, or things spoken about. *I asked **them** for a ride. I waited for **them** for twenty minutes.*

**these** ***These** spelling words are really easy!* Look up **this.**

**they** People other than yourself. ***They** are my friends.*

**thing** *plural* **things.** An object that may not need to be named. *What is this **thing** used for?*

**think** To use the mind. ***Think** about what you are going to say before you say it.* **thought, thinking** *I am **thinking** about the story I just read.*

**this** *plural* **these.** Something here and not there. *Anna, look at **this** spaceship.*

**three** *plural* **threes.** The number after two, written 3. *Two plus one equals **three.***

**tie** **1.** *plural* **ties.** A necktie. *He spilled something on his **tie.*** **2.** An equal score. *The pie-eating contest ended in a **tie.*** **3.** To attach something with string or rope. *She tried to **tie** Mei's shoelaces together.* **tied, tying**

**tiger** *plural* **tigers.** A large wild cat that lives in Asia. ***Tigers** have brown-yellow fur and black stripes.*

**tiny** Very small. *Greta wants a **tiny** piano for her doll house.* **tinier, tiniest**

**to** **1.** Toward. *The bus broke down on the way **to** school.* **2.** For. *It is important **to** me.*

**today** This day. ***Today** is my birthday!*

**told** *We all* **told** *about our vacations in school yesterday.* Look up **tell.**

**too** Also. *In a thunderstorm, there is rain and lightning. Sometimes there is hail,* **too.**

**took** *The bus driver* **took** *our tickets.* Look up **take.**

**tooth** *plural* **teeth.** A hard, white bony growth in the mouth. *My* **tooth** *is loose.*

**top** *plural* **tops.** The highest part. *What time is it when an elephant sits on* **top** *of a fence? (Time to get a new fence.)*

**torch** *plural* **torches.** **1.** A burning light on a stick that can be carried. *The parade was at night. Dad carried a big* **torch.** **2.** A tool that shoots out fire. *She used a* **torch** *to make the metal soft.*

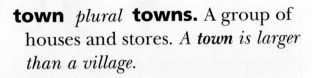

**town** *plural* **towns.** A group of houses and stores. *A* **town** *is larger than a village.*

**train 1.** *plural* **trains.** An engine with a line of cars after it. *We take the* **train** *to visit our cousins.* **2.** To teach. *When you have a dog, you must* **train** *it to mind you.* **trained, training**

**tread** To walk. *Please do not* **tread** *on the grass.* **trod, treading**

**trick 1.** *plural* **tricks.** A thing that fools someone. *On April Fool's Day, I played a* **trick.** *I told my mother there was an elephant in the bathtub.* **2.** To fool someone. *I will* **trick** *her again next year. I will tell her that there is a lion in the yard.* **tricked, tricking** *Carlos* **tricked** *me by wearing a wig.*

**truck** *plural* **trucks.** A vehicle used to carry heavy loads. *Oranges are sent by* **truck** *from Florida to Vermont.*

**try 1.** To work hard at something. *Try not to make a mistake on your spelling test!* **2.** To test something. *Would you like to* **try** *my bike?* **tried, trying**

**two** *plural* **twos.** The number after one, written 2. *One plus one is* **two.**

**tying** *Eddie is* **tying** *the string around his finger.* Look up **tie.**

**under** Beneath. *Pat and I walked* **under** *my umbrella.*

**up** From low to high. *What's red and goes* **up** *and down? (A tomato in an elevator)*

**us** The speaker and one or more other people. *May Roger leave his hamsters with* **us** *over the summer?*

**van** *plural* **vans.** A covered truck or wagon. *He took the children to the picnic in his van.*

**very** Extremely. *Dinosaurs lived on earth a very long time ago.*

**wait** To stay until something happens. *We had to wait a long time for the movie to begin.* **waited, waiting**

**walk** To move ahead by foot. *We will walk to the store.* **walked, walking**

**want** To wish for. *People want peace in the world.* **wanted, wanting**

**was** *Blackbeard was a famous pirate.* Look up **be.**

**wash** To clean with water or other liquid and often with soap. *You should always wash your hands before you eat.* **washed, washing**

**we** The speaker and one or more other people. *We had fun at the circus.*

**week** *plural* **weeks.** Seven days, starting with Sunday and ending Saturday. *My cousins are going to visit us for a week.*

**well 1.** *plural* **wells.** Deep hole dug in the ground. *We get wonderful water from the well in our yard.* **2.** Pleasing, good. *Your homework was done very well.*

**went** *Linda went to get the bike.* Look up **go.**

**whale** *plural* **whales.** A large air-breathing sea animal. *A whale is a mammal, not a fish.*

**what** Which thing. *What is gray and white and red all over? (A sunburned elephant)*

**when** At what time. *When will you be home?*

**white** *plural* **whites.** The lightest of all colors. *White is the color of snow and clouds.*

**who 1.** Which person. *Who is the man ringing our doorbell?* **2.** That. *He is the person who teaches music at school.*

**why** For what reason. *Why do people sneeze?*

**will 1.** Going to. *I will come to your house after school.* **2.** Must. *You will clean your room.* **would**

**wind** *plural* **winds.** Air that blows. *It's fun to fly our kites in the wind.*

**wish 1.** *plural* **wishes.** A strong desire. *My* **wish** *is that it will not rain on Saturday.* **2.** To want. *I* **wish** *that we could go to the parade on Saturday.* **wished, wishing** *He* **wished** *that he could get a new hamster.*

**with 1.** Having. *My favorite shirt is the one* **with** *buttons on the collar.* **2.** In the company of. *Will you come fishing* **with** *me?*

**would** *They said they* **would** *come to the party.* Look up **will.**

**write** To make words with pencil, chalk, or other tools. *Meg likes to* **write** *in her diary every day.*

**wrote, writing** *We are* **writing** *letters to our pen pals.*

**writer** *plural* **writers.** Someone who writes stories or poems. *I like to read all of Glen's stories. He is a good* **writer.**

**yellow** *plural* **yellows.** The color of a ripe lemon. *Yellow is the color I use to draw the sun.*

**yes** I agree. *Yes, I would like to go to the circus!*

**you** Person or persons spoken to. *You are my best friend.*

**zoo** *plural* **zoos.** A place where animals are kept. *You can learn a lot about wild animals by visiting a* **zoo.**